THE DIARY
OF TOLSTOY'S WIFE

THE DIARY OF TOLSTOY'S WIFE
1860-1891

Translated from the Russian by

ALEXANDER WERTH

NEW YORK
PAYSON AND CLARKE LTD

Printed in Great Britain

CONTENTS

PREFACE

The original Russian text, of which the present volume is a complete translation, was published by M. and S. Sabashnikov, Moscow, in September, 1928, under the general title of *Dnevniki Sofyi Andreyevny Tolstoy* (*1860–91*) (*The Diaries of Sophie Andreyevna Tolstoy*).

In addition to the author's *Diary* covering the period from 1862 to 1891, and published now for the first time, this volume contains (1) a retrospective account of her engagement and marriage, in 1862, written two years after Tolstoy's death, (2) the only surviving fragment of a diary kept by her before her marriage, (3) a collection of extremely valuable notes on Tolstoy's literary life, headed "Notes for Future Reference," (4) a story of the "origin" of Anna Karenina's death, and (5) the story of Tolstoy's quarrel with Turgenev. The actual *Diary* is probably the most valuable first-hand document in existence on Tolstoy's family life, and explains more clearly than anything yet published the various psychological factors that underlay that famous "unhappy marriage." But was the marriage altogether unhappy? The *Diary* suggests clearly enough that it was; yet it must be remembered that, although it covers a period of twenty-eight years, it contains no more than 233 entries, an average of one entry in six weeks. Indeed, at some periods no more than one or two entries a year were made, and it has been rightly suggested that Countess Tolstoy had recourse to her diary only when she felt particularly angry or depressed. It would therefore be wrong to conclude that Tolstoy's marriage was one continuous tale of woe. We know from his own writings that this was not the case, and that he knew what real family happiness meant, especially during the earlier years of his marriage. This *Diary*, however, shows that even then the seeds of discord were present, and there was one element in the tragedy which is revealed here with particular clearness—Sophie Andreyevna's very strong feeling of class-consciousness. " He disgusts me with his People," she wrote during the very first year of her marriage. And when, later, after Tolstoy's conversion, Yasnaya Polyana became the meeting-place of all kinds of " dark," disreputable plebeians, the constant presence of these people, much more than Tolstoy's new attitude to life, drove Sophie Andreyevna at times to the highest pitch of irritation. She never forgot, and hated Tolstoy to forget, that he was a count.

At the same time it must be remembered (what a supreme touch of irony !) that it was thanks to Sophie Andreyevna's perseverance and personal influence in government circles that in 1890 the ban was removed from the *Kreutzer Sonata* ! In spite of everything, she tried to remain his helpmate to the end.

A. W.

London,

October, 1928.

A TRIP TO THE TROITZA MONASTERY

(The only surviving fragment of Countess Tolstoy's Diary written before her Marriage)

A TRIP TO THE TROITZA MONASTERY

(The only surviving fragment of Countess Tolstoy's Diary written before her Marriage)

June 14, 1860.

We set out at four in the morning, sleepy and in a bad mood. Luba[1] and I got inside the charabanc, Mother sat in front, and the two Lisas[2] and Sasha[3] travelled in the cart. We drowsed and were silent all the way. Only once the monotony of the journey was broken by an outburst of laughter coming from the cart. At Mytishchi the usual crowd of peasant women surrounded us, offering us tea beneath the birch-trees and assuring us that we ought to try some Mytishchi water. We arrived at Bratovshchina at 9 a.m., as expected, and stopped at the best inn. As soon as we arrived, we opened up the lunch parcels, and finished off a whole mushroom-pie in no time. Then they brought in the samovar. In the meantime I examined the pictures hanging on the walls. These included portraits of the Emperor, the Empress, and the Metropolitan of the Church, two paintings with French inscriptions, and two religious pictures.

Sasha is now lying down and busy reading the *Funny Calendar*. The Petersburg Lisa and Luba are fussing with the food, Mother washing dishes, and our Lisa getting in everybody's way, begging for food and trying to pinch some caramels out of the bag.

After tea, Luba and I went out to ask a peasant why a chapel had been built here. He entered the hut and told us a long story of how in 1812 the church here had been moved to another spot, and how they were going to build a public-house in its place, and how the priest and the church elder had reported the matter to the Metropolitan. The Metropolitan forbade it, and ordered a chapel to be built on the spot where the church had stood.

We have just been allowed to go for a bathe. The innkeeper's daughter, a girl of seventeen, will take us to the River Skalda. Her father, a very talkative peasant, started a whole philosophic argument about her, telling us how hard it was to get one's daughters married, how difficult it was to know people, and how deceitful they were. He was quite right, and showed real good Russian common sense. He said that it was their custom to pay a father for his daughter, and that the father, in his turn, had to supply the daughter with a dowry.

We are going to have a rest now, but I don't suppose we'll be able to sleep. Then we shall have a bathe, have dinner, and drive away at 4 p.m. All the time I longed for some travelling companions, and at last my wish came true. There were some other people having tea behind the thin wooden partition ; these were a fat gentleman, a lady of equal dimensions, a wizened old woman, and a blonde little girl. They all kept unusually silent—not at all a cheerful company. I was much amused watching them get out of their *brichka*. The innkeeper brought along a bench to help them to get out, and it was amusing to see how they all groaned as they stumbled out of the carriage. I am tired of this place ; I wish we would leave soon. And I'm feeling generally depressed. Nothing seems to cheer me, as in the old days. I try to distract myself, but my head is full of dismal thoughts.

We did as we intended. We left Bratovshchina at four. Luba, Sasha, and I got into the cart, while the others took their seats in the charabanc. On the way we carried on a cheerful, or, rather, a pleasant, conversation. We stopped at the chapel and had some pancakes. There we talked to the village girls, who crowded round in large numbers. They asked us how we were related to each other, whether there were any married girls among us, when we would come back, and saw us off with every kind of blessing and good wish, saying that they had seldom seen such friendly gentlefolk.

We reached Troitza‘ at nine in the evening and were given a large, decent room with a fine view of the monastery. The weather is fine, calm, and warm, and inclines one to meditation. The Troitza Monastery made a curious impression on me this time. I never drove into its precincts before with such a feeling of faith and devotion. That's the result of sorrow. I believe that, if I pray, all my cares and sorrows will vanish. It's quite true that "faith saves." Although these reflections may seem funny, what can I do when faith and prayer are my only consolation ? I have put my trust in God, and shall now tread my path with closed eyes, trusting in His help and blessing. Life is a hard thing, and I am no good at guiding myself. How often have I made good and firm resolutions, yet each time my powers have failed me and

I have had to abandon my intentions. But I'm becoming too pensive. I've got such a queer, silly temperament.

Everybody around me is fussing and rushing about ; we have just had tea and are getting ready for bed. Luba has prepared her bed next to mine. All the things are packed up, and we shall soon go to sleep. I keep on thinking of the young lady I saw standing in front of the hotel. She was all in mourning and held a new-born baby in her arms, probably her daughter, for she was the very image of her mother. This lady must have lost her husband—that was the first thought that occurred to me—I wonder why. She was very beautiful and dark—quite to my taste—but so sad and miserable that I felt very sorry for her. I seem to feel sad all the time, and am always pitying someone ; and my head is full of gloomy thoughts. How can I get rid of them ? I shall go to bed presently. Luba is calling.

June 15, 1860.

We got up at seven this morning, and Mother had all the trouble in the world to get me and Luba out of bed. We slept together, having arranged a double bed, and everybody made fun of us, calling us a married couple. I called Luba my husband and kept on kissing her.

When we got up we had tea and then went to Mass. We walked around the place, looking at all the things of interest, and pointing out all the remarkable churches, buildings, etc., to our cousins. We attended Mass at St. Sergius's Church. The singing was fine, and one of the monks gave a rather good sermon on faith and piety. Here we met Golovin, and went for a stroll with him. We walked all round the place, saw everything worth seeing, and bought a lot of little ikons, toys, and other presents to take home. Then we went to bathe in the pond at the theological students' cabin ; but the water there was vile. It's half-past two now, and we are going to dine. We'll start out home about four. Should I be glad or sad to go home ? I feel so bored, so depressed that everything seems wrong to me.

Evening of June 15, 1860.

We are on our way home. We left Troitza ; Golovin saw us off and was very nice and pleasant. We stopped at Talitsa, where we had a stroll around the caves. It is so damp and cold there, and the vaults are so low, that I was sorry I had gone. I sat in front, driving the horses myself, to the great amusement of the passers-by. When we reached Bratovshchina and stopped at the same inn, we called in a large number of boys and girls and made them sing. We had plenty of fun with them, and they managed to cheer me up. Only it is a pity that all the boys who had got some money from us promptly went off to play pitch-and-toss. Their passion for gambling begins too early in life. Later on a gentleman staying at another inn made them sing more songs. After tea Luba and I went for a stroll along the road. There are always lots of things to see in a village. The innkeeper's brother-in-law drove past us, looking quite drunk. The innkeeper himself, equally drunk, was walking in front of the house, cursing, rolling about, and talking a lot of nonsense. The women merely complain and cry. The older ones are more used to it, and bear it in silence.

Our innkeeper's sister-in-law said there were very few sober husbands nowadays. When there's an inn or a public-house in the place, it isn't to be wondered at. I spoke to her, sitting on the bench behind the gate, and played with her little girl, Tanya, a pretty, fair child of four. She is a lively, clever little creature, and I made her pronounce French words, which she did very funnily. I'm going to bed now. Lisa, Mother, Luba, and the other Lisa are already in bed. It is ten now, and we shall start at two in the morning, or, rather, at night. I can hear Sasha snoring behind the wall, and Mother is envying him ; Luba has also fallen asleep. The three of us—Luba, the Petersburg Lisa, and myself—have spread some hay on the floor and have covered it with a carpet and some sheets, and are going to sleep on it.

On our way we shall stop for tea at Mytishchi, at 8 or 9 a.m. I'm not glad to be going home—I simply don't care. I would rather go somewhere far away, or even drop into some dark pit and die ; only to forget what happened. I was so happy, so joyful, but it didn't last long, and life is very cruel to me now. I'm afraid to live on memories ; I dare not. I try to forget, and yet I am not strong enough to do it. What can I do ? How must I act ? I try everything in vain, like a bird in a cage. I may well quote Lermontov :

I am weary and sad,
And not a friendly hand . . .

If only there were a friendly hand I could take, if only there were someone who could give me some good, helpful advice !

We had tea and coffee at Mytishchi at six. Now we are back home. I'm very glad to find everyone cheerful and well.

L. N. TOLSTOY'S MARRIAGE

(Countess Tolstoy's Reminiscences written in 1912)

L. N. TOLSTOY'S MARRIAGE

(*Countess Tolstoy's Reminiscences written in 1912*)

OUR TRIP TO IVITSY AND YASNAYA POLYANA

At the beginning of August 1862, my two sisters and I were overjoyed to hear that Mother had decided to go by Annenkov's coach to her father's estate, and to take Volodya,[5] our little brother, and the three of us with her.

At this time our grandfather, Alexander Mikhailovich Islenyev[6] (the " papa " of Lev Nikolaevich's *Childhood*) lived on his Ivitsy estate in the Odoevsky district. Ivitsy was the last remnant of what had once been a large fortune, and even it had been bought in the name of his second wife, my mother's stepmother, Sophie Alexandrovna, *née* Zhdanov—the woman who figures in Lev Nikolaevich's *Childhood* as *la belle Flamande*.

The three daughters[7] of my grandfather's second marriage were quite young girls in those days, and I was very friendly with the second one.

My grandfather's estate was about forty miles from Yasnaya Polyana. Maria Nikolaevna[8] (Lev's sister) had just returned from Algeria, and as my mother and she had been the greatest friends in their childhood, my mother was naturally anxious to see her again. Nor had she been in Yasnaya since her childhood, and so she decided to call there on our way to Ivitsy. This delighted us even more, since Tanya[9] and I, like all young people, were only too glad to see as many places and people as possible. The preparations were lively, and smart new dresses were made for us ; we packed our luggage and waited anxiously for the day of departure.

I hardly remember the actual departure. Nor are my recollections of the journey very clear—all I remember is that we stopped at inns, changed horses, hurried through our meals, and grew very tired towards the end of the journey. We stopped at Tula to see my mother's sister, Nadezhda Alexandrovna Karnovich, who was married to the Tula Leader of the Nobility. We had a look at Tula, which struck me as being a dirty, dull, uninteresting town. Only we didn't want to *miss* anything, and were determined to look carefully at everything on our way.

After dinner we drove to Yasnaya Polyana. It was already late, but the evening was glorious. The main road, which passes through the Zaseka forest, is so picturesque, and the scenery so vast and spacious, that it seemed to us, city girls that we were, like a piece of primitive nature.

Maria Nikolaevna and Lev Nikolaevich greeted us in a most jovial manner. Aunt Tatiana Alexandrovna Ergolsky,[10] a reserved but pleasant woman, greeted us in cordially-polite French fashion, and her companion, old Nathalie Petrovna, silently stroked me on the shoulder and winked cheerfully at Tanya, my younger sister, who was then only fifteen.

We were given a large vaulted room on the ground floor, modestly and even poorly furnished. There were white-painted sofas against the walls, with hard backs and seats covered with striped blue-and-white canvas, and there was also a *chaise-longue*, painted and upholstered in the same way. The table was of rough birch-wood, made by the local cabinet-maker. There were large iron rings hanging from the ceiling, which in the old days were used for holding saddles, hams, etc. This room had been a store-room in the days of Prince Volkonsky,[11] Lev Nikolaevich's grandfather.

It was the beginning of August, and the days were growing short. After we had run round the garden, Nathalie Petrovna took us to see the raspberry bushes. I had never eaten raspberries off the bush, but only out of the baskets which were brought to our country house during the jam season. There were very few berries on the bushes, but I loved the beauty of the red against the green leaves, and greatly enjoyed their fresh taste.

THE NIGHT AND THE ARMCHAIR

As it was growing dark, Mother sent me down to unpack the luggage and to get the beds ready. Dunyasha (Auntie's maid) and I were preparing the beds, when Lev Nikolaevich suddenly walked into the room. Dunyasha told him that she had arranged three beds on the sofas, but that there was no room for a fourth one.

"Why not try the armchair?" said Lev Nikolaevich, and clumsily began to unfold a sheet. I felt a little embarrassed, but at the same time there was something nice and intimate in the way in which he helped us to arrange the beds.

When everything was ready, we went upstairs and found Tanya rolled up on the little sofa in Auntie's room, fast asleep. Volodya also had been put to bed. Mother was talking of the old days to Maria Nikolaevna and Auntie. Lisa looked questioningly at us. I can clearly remember every moment of that evening.

In the dining-room, with its big Italian window, Alexey Stepanovich, the little squint-eyed butler, was laying the table for supper. Dunyasha, a majestic, handsome girl (the daughter of old Nicholas of *Childhood* fame) helped him in arranging the table. The door in the middle of the wall was open, and led into a little drawing-room with an antique rosewood clavichord, and the drawing-room door, with the same kind of Italian window, led on to a little balcony. This balcony had a charming view which I have loved all my life. It gives me joy to this day.

I took a chair, and, going out on to the balcony, I admired the sight. I shall never forget the emotions I felt that evening, though I shall never be able to describe them. Was it the effect of the country, of nature, of this feeling of spaciousness? Was it a presentiment of what was to happen six weeks later, when I became the mistress of this house? Was it simply a farewell to the free days of girlhood? I cannot tell. But there was something new and significant in my mood that evening, something rapturous and hitherto inexperienced. Everybody assembled for supper. Lev Nikolaevich came to call me, too.

"No, thank you, I don't want to eat," I said; "it's so fine out here."

From the dining-room I could hear the unnatural, playful voice of my sister Tanya—a spoilt child, and always expecting to be spoilt. Lev Nikolaevich returned to the dining-room, but, before finishing his supper, he came back to the balcony. I can't remember exactly what we talked about; I only remember how he said to me, "How serene and simple you are." I liked that very much.

I slept well in the long armchair which Lev Nikolaevich had prepared for me. At first I tossed about for a little, for the two arms made it a little narrow and uncomfortable; but my heart was full of joy and laughter as I thought of Lev Nikolaevich preparing my bed for me, and I soon fell asleep, with a new feeling of joy in my whole youthful being.

THE PICNIC AT YASNAYA POLYANA

My awakening the next morning was joyful. I longed to run round the place, to look at everything, to talk to everybody. How alive and airy everything seemed in Yasnaya Polyana, even in those days! Lev Nikolaevich did everything to keep us amused, and Maria Nikolaevna supported him in every way. Lev Nikolaevich ordered a carriage with two horses, and had the grey Belogubka harnessed with an old-fashioned lady's saddle. A very fine white horse was saddled for him, too, and we began to get ready for the picnic.

Some other visitors arrived—Mme. Gromov, the wife of a Tula architect, and Sonya Bergholz, a niece of Julia Feodorovna Auerbach, the head mistress of the girls' high school in Tula. Maria Nikolaevna, who was happy to have her two best friends—my mother and Mme. Gromov—with her, was in a particularly playful and happy mood; she joked and laughed and kept us all cheerful. Lev Nikolaevich asked me if I would ride Belogubka, which I was very anxious to do.

"Yes, but I haven't a riding habit," said I, looking at my yellow dress with its black velvet belt and buttons.

"That doesn't matter," said Lev Nikolaevich, with a smile. "There are no villas here ; no one except the trees of the wood will see you," he added, helping me into the saddle.

No one could have been happier than me as I galloped beside Lev Nikolaevich, along the road leading to the Zaseka wood, our first stopping-place ; in those days it was still all forest. When, later on, I drove to these places, they never again seemed quite the same to me. That morning everything was different ; it all seemed full of magic, as it never does in ordinary life, but only in certain moods of spiritual exaltation. We came to a little meadow with a haystack in the middle. In later years, Tanya's family and my own had many a picnic in that meadow, but it was quite different then, and I looked at it with different eyes.

Maria Nikolaevna invited us all to climb up the haystack and to roll down, which we all gladly did. We spent a noisy and merry evening.

The next morning we drove to Krasnoye, a village that had once belonged to my grandfather, Islenyev. My grandmother is buried there. Mother was very anxious to visit the spot where she was born and had spent her childhood, and to pay homage to her mother's grave, beside the church. At Yasnaya they were all very sorry to see us go, and made Mother swear that we would call again on our way home, if only for a day.

KRASNOYE

We drove to Krasnoye in Maria Nikolaevna's carriage, but with hired horses. We didn't stay there long.

I remember the church, and the tombstone with its inscription : " Princess Sophie Petrovna Kozlovsky, born Countess Zavadovsky." I clearly pictured my grandmother's life—the terrible time she had with that drunkard, Kozlovsky, her first husband, whom she married against her will ; her illegal marriage with Alexander Mikhailovich Islenyev, my grandfather ; her life in this village atmosphere, with her uninterrupted yearly succession of children, and her constant fear that my grandfather, obsessed with the gambling mania, would lose his entire fortune and have to leave his estate—which, indeed, did happen towards the end of his life. The old priest and Fetis, the little deacon, still remembered my grandmother, and spoke very warmly of her. " I committed a sin and married them in secret," the old priest told us. " She begged me so much to do it for her : ' If not in the eyes of men, at least in the eyes of God, I want to be Alexander Mikhailovich's wife.' " We also heard a story of how Fetis, the little deacon, had, in the middle of his own funeral, suddenly jumped out of the coffin and walked home. I can still see his dried-up little figure, and the grey little pigtail at the back of his head. I had never seen a deacon with a pigtail in Moscow, and nothing had ever given me such a surprise. Everything that day seemed fantastic and full of beautiful magic.

IVITSY

After feeding the horses at Krasnoye, we drove on in the same carriage to Ivitsy, my grandfather's estate. The reception was joyful and solemn. Gliding rapidly along the floor in his soft little boots, grandfather kept joking with us, and calling us "the young Moscow ladies." He had a habit of pinching our cheeks with his middle finger and his forefinger, and of blinking at us cheerfully with his half-closed little eyes. I can still see his powerful figure and the little black skull-cap on his bald head, his aquiline nose, and his clean-shaven, rosy face. Sophie Alexandrovna, his second wife, always amazed us by smoking a long pipe, her lower lip hanging down while she did it. Only her expressive, bright, black eyes remained to tell of her former beauty.

The handsome Olga, their second daughter, cold and placid to look at, took us upstairs to our room. My bed was behind the cupboard, and, instead of a table, they gave me a plain wooden chair.

The next day we were taken round to see some neighbours. We got to know some young girls, all very pleasant, but quite different from us in every way. Those were real country maidens of the Turgenev type. The life of the landowners in those days was still full of the old serf-owning spirit. Their habits were very simple ; they did without railroads and their interests were confined to their immediate surroundings—their farms, their neighbours, their hunting parties, handicrafts, and, now and then, some simple, cheerful church or family celebrations. Our arrival in the

Odoevsky district created something of a stir. Many people came to have a look at us, and arranged picnics, dances, and excursions for our benefit.

The day following our arrival in Ivitsy, Lev Nikolaevich turned up unexpectedly on his white horse. He had done forty miles, but was full of vigour and joyful excitement. My grandfather, who was fond of Lev Nikolaevich, and of the whole Tolstoy family in general—for he had been a friend of Count Nicholas Ilyich[11]—greeted Lev Nikolaevich in the most affectionate manner. There were rather a lot of visitors. After the day's excursion, the young people arranged to have a dance at night. There were some officers among them, some young squires from the neighbourhood, and a lot of young ladies and girls. To us they were a crowd of strangers. But hat did it matter? It was very jolly, and that was the main thing. Different people took their turn at the piano.

"How smart you all are!" Lev Nikolaevich remarked, looking at my white-and-mauve dress, with its lilac ribbons falling from the shoulders—a fashion known in those days as *suivez-moi*. "It's a pity Auntie isn't here to see how smart you can look," he said, with a smile.

"Aren't you dancing?" I asked.

"Oh, no; I'm far too old for that."

During the evening some elderly men and ladies had been playing cards at two tables. These tables, with the candles still burning, were left open even after all the visitors were gone. We stayed on in the drawing-room for some time, listening to Lev Nikolaevich's lively talk. But Mother thought we ought to go to bed, and told us firmly to do so. We did not dare disobey her. But, as I was about to leave the room, Lev Nikolaevich suddenly called me :

" Wait a minute, Sophie Andreyevna ! "

" What's the matter ? "

" Try to read what I'll write."

" Very well," said I.

"But I shall only write the initials."

" How's that ? But that'll be impossible ! Well, go on ! "

Lev Nikolaevich brushed the game scores off the card-table, and, taking a bit of chalk, began to write. We were both very solemn and excited. I watched his large red hand, and felt how all my thoughts and feelings were concentrated on the piece of chalk and on the hand that was holding it. We were both silent.

WHAT THE CHALK WROTE[13]

" Y. y. & y. d. f. h. r. m. t. v. o. m. o. a. & o. m. i. f. h."

" Your youth and your desire for happiness remind me too vividly of my old age and of my incapacity for happiness," I read out.

My heart began to throb violently, my face was flushed, and I seemed to have suddenly lost all sense of time and reality ; I felt as though at that moment I could grasp everything, conceive the inconceivable.

" Well, let's try again," said Lev Nikolaevich, and wrote :

" Y. f. h. f. i. a. m. & y. s. L. W. y. & y. s. T. p. m."

" Your family have false ideas about me and your sister Lisa. Won't you and your sister Tanya protect me?" I read out rapidly, without hesitating for a second. Lev Nikolaevich wasn't even surprised; it somehow seemed perfectly natural. Our state of mind was so tense and exalted that nothing seemed to surprise us.

I heard Mother's peevish voice telling me to go to bed. We said good night hastily, put out the lights, and departed. Behind the cupboard upstairs I lighted a candle-end and, sitting on the floor, with my note-book on the wooden chair in front of me, I started writing my diary.

I at once wrote down the sentences of which Lev Nikolaevich had given me the initials, and suddenly felt that something serious and important had taken place between us—something that wouldn't stop there. But for various reasons I checked my thoughts on the subject. It was as though I was locking up for a while all that had happened during that evening.

We spent another day at Yasnaya Polyana on our way back from Ivitsy. But it wasn't so jolly this time. Maria Nikolaevna intended to go with us to Moscow, and thence abroad, where she had left her children, and Aunt Tatiana Alexandrovna, who loved her "Mashenka" passionately, was silent and sad. Maria's absence always made her melancholy; Aunt Tatiana had brought her up from childhood, loved her like a child of her own, and pitied her for her unhappy life with her husband, Count Valerian Petrovitch Tolstoy, who—to make matters worse—was Aunt Tatiana's own nephew, being the son of her sister, Elizabeth Alexandrovna. Lev Nikolaevich's attitude towards me, and the suspicious looks that my sisters and the others were giving me, made it all rather uncomfortable for me. Mother, too, seemed to be worried about something, while Tànya and little Volodya were growing tired of the journey and were longing to be home again.

THE JOURNEY IN THE ANNENSKY COACH

We sent to Tula for a large Annensky coach (named thus after the owner's name). There were four seats inside and two at the back, the latter resembling those of a two-wheeler with a hood. My sisters and I were leaving Yasnaya with many regrets. We said good-bye to Auntie and Nathalie Petrovna, and went to look for Lev Nikolaevich to take leave of him too.

" I am going with you," he said simply and cheerfully. " How can I stay in Yasnaya now ? It'll be so dull and lonely."

Without realising why, I suddenly began to feel very happy. I ran to announce the news to my mother and sisters. It was decided that Lev Nikolaevich would travel all the way outside, while Lisa and I would take the other outside seat in turns.

And so we drove on and on. . . . In the evening I began to feel chilly, and wrapped myself up in my cloak, and a feeling of quiet happiness overcame me as I sat there beside the old friend of my family, the beloved author of *Childhood*, who now seemed more kind and friendly than ever. He kept telling me lovely long stories of the Caucasus, of his life there, of the beauty of its mountains, of its primitive nature, and of his own exploits. I felt so happy, listening to his calm, even slightly hoarse voice, which sounded so tender, as though it were coming from a distance. I would fall asleep for a moment, but, starting up, I would again hear the same voice continuing its poetic Caucasian story. I was ashamed of my sleepiness, but I was so young then, and, although it was a pity to miss any of Lev Nikolaevich's stories, I was at times unable to overcome my weariness. We travelled all night. Inside the coach everybody was asleep, and only now and then Mother and Maria Nikolaevna would exchange a few words, or little Volodya would cry in his sleep.

At last we reached the outskirts of Moscow, and it was once again my turn to sit outside next to Lev Nikolaevich. At the last halt Lisa came up to me and begged me to let her ride outside.

" Sonya, if you don't mind—will you let me have the outside seat? It's so stuffy inside the coach!" she said. We came out of the waiting-room and I took my seat inside the coach.

" Sophie Andreyevna!" Lev Nikolaevich cried, " it's your turn now to sit outside."

" I know, but I'm cold," said I elusively. And the carriage door closed with a thump.

Lev Nikolaevich stood there for a moment with a thoughtful air, and then climbed up to his seat.

The next day Maria Nikolaevna went abroad, and we returned to our country house at Pokzovskoye, where my father and brothers[14] were expecting us.

THE LAST DAYS OF GIRLHOOD AND A STORY

My whole life had changed. To all appearances, it was the same—the same people, the same surroundings.

But my personal independence seemed to have disappeared ; the feeling that had taken a hold on me in Ivitsy and Yasnaya Polyana continued to grow. A powerful sense of infinite freedom seemed to have absorbed my ego. I was living those last days of my girlhood with a particularly vivid sense of life, illuminated with a strange inner light, as though my soul had suddenly awakened. Only on two other occasions in my life did I have this same sense of spiritual exaltation. These rare awakenings of the soul have done more than anything else to convince me that the soul lives an independent life of its own, that the soul is immortal and that with death it regains its freedom.

Having followed us to Moscow from Yasnaya Polyana, Lev Nikolaevich took a room at some German shoemaker's house and settled down there. In those days he was busy with his Yasnaya Polyana school and with a magazine called *Yasnaya Polyana*, an educational kind of paper, meant to be used in peasant schools. It only lasted a year. Lev Nikolaevich came to Pokrovskoye nearly every day to see us. Sometimes my father, who often went to Moscow in connection with his duties, would bring him back with him. One day Lev Nikolaevich told us that he had called at the Peter Park Palace and had handed the A.D.C. on duty a letter to the Emperor Alexander II regarding the insult he had suffered through the search made by the *gendarmerie* at Yasnaya Polyana.[11] He told us this on August 23, 1862. The Emperor was then staying at the Peter Palace in Moscow in connection with the Khodynka manœuvres.

Lev Nikolaevich and I often went for walks and talked a great deal ; and once he asked me if I kept a diary. I told him I had kept one ever since I was eleven, and that I had also written a long story last summer, when I was sixteen.

"Let me read your diaries," Lev Nikolaevich asked.

"No, I can't."

"Well, let me see the story, then."

This I gave him. The next morning I asked him whether he had read it. He said calmly and indifferently, that he had glanced through it. Later on I read in his diary the following entry about my story: "She let me read her story. What a powerful sense of truth and simplicity!" And he later also told me that he hadn't slept that night, and had felt very much excited about my reflections on one of the characters (Prince Dublitsky), in whom he had recognised himself and of whom I had said: "The Prince had a remarkably attractive appearance, but his views were inconstant."

We were once, I remember, in a particularly merry and playful mood, and I kept on repeating the same silly remark: "When I become Empress, I'll do this or that," or "When I become Empress, I'll order this or that." My father's empty cabriolet was standing near the balcony at that time. The horse had just been taken to the stable. I jumped into the carriage and cried: "When I become Empress, I'll drive about in this kind of cabriolet."

No sooner did Lev Nikolaevich hear it than he seized the shafts, and, pulling hard, drove me along at a quick trot. "I'm going to give my Empress a drive," he said. (This shows how strong and healthy he was at the time.) "Don't, don't! It's too heavy for you!" I cried, though I felt happy to see how strong he was, and was really only too delighted to be pulled along like this. How wonderful the moonlit nights were that year! I can still see the little meadow bathed in moonlight, with the moon reflected in the pond close by. Those were fresh, bracing, August nights. "What a mad night!" Lev Nikolaevich would say, as we sat on the balcony or walked about the garden. We didn't have any romantic scenes or declarations. We already knew each other so well. It was as though I were trying to end as beautifully as possible the free, serene, and careless years of my girlhood. Everything seemed so lovely and free of care; I had no desires, and the future seemed of no importance.

Again and again Lev Nikolaevich would come to see us. Sometimes, when he stayed very late, my parents would put him up for the night. Once, at the very beginning of September, we went to see him off, and, when the time arrived to say good-bye to him, Lisa commissioned me to invite him to her name-day party on September 5. I invited him very insistently; at first he refused, and asked me: "Why are you so particular about the 5th?" I didn't dare to explain; I had been told not to mention the name-day at all.

In the end Lev Nikolaevich promised to come, and, much to our joy, he kept his word. He always made everything so jolly and interesting.

At first I did not connect his visits with myself. But I gradually realised that he was beginning to count in my life. One day, in a state of great excitement, I ran upstairs to our room with its Italian window, from which I could see the pond, the church, and all the things I had loved since my earliest days (I was born at Pokrovskoye), and as I stood at the window my heart beat violently. Tanya came in, and at once realised how restless I was.

"What's the matter, Sonya ?" she asked sympathetically.

"Je crains d'aimer le comte," said I in a calm and dry tone of voice. "No ? Really ?" she said in surprise—for she had never suspected it. She even grew quite sad, for she knew my temperament.

Never, indeed, throughout my life, has *aimer* meant an emotional game to me, but always something very much akin to suffering.

IN MOSCOW

Between the 5th and the 16th the whole family moved to Moscow. As usual, after leaving the country house and all the beauties of nature, Moscow felt so dull and narrow and depressing that it had quite a bad effect on my frame of mind. Before leaving the country we always used to say good-bye to as many of our favourite haunts as possible. That autumn, indeed, I paid my final farewell to Pokrovskoye, as well as to my years of girlhood. In Moscow, Lev Nikolaevich resumed his frequent visits. One evening I went on tiptoe into Mother's bedroom. How often did Mother, after our return from a party or a theatre, cheerfully say, "Well, my dear, tell me all about it." And then I would give her a long account of the evening, and try to impersonate all I had seen at the theatre. But this time neither of us was very cheerful.

"Well, Sonya ?" she asked.

" Listen, Mother. Everybody thinks that it isn't *me* whom Lev Nikolaevich wants to marry, and yet I believe he loves me," said I timidly.

For some reason Mother grew angry, and pounced on me. " You always imagine that everybody's in love with you," said she angrily. " Go away and don't think such nonsense."

I was much hurt by my mother's attitude to my candid admission, and after that I didn't again mention Lev Nikolaevich to anybody. Father, too, was angry that Lev Nikolaevich, in spite of his frequent visits, hadn't proposed to the eldest daughter—as the old Russian custom demanded—and began to treat him very coldly, and was also rather unkind to me. The atmosphere of the house was becoming strained and uncomfortable—especially for me.

On September 14, Lev Nikolaevich said that he had something very important to tell me, but he didn't have time to say what it was. It was easy enough to guess. He spoke to me at great length during that evening. I played the piano in the drawing-room, while he, leaning heavily on the mantelpiece, kept saying each time I stopped : " Go on, go on ! " The music prevented the others from hearing what he was saying, and my hands trembled with excitement and my fingers stumbled over the keys as I played for the tenth time the same tune from the *Baccio* waltz. I had learned it by heart in order to accompany Tanya's singing.

Lev Nikolaevich didn't propose that evening, and I don't remember very clearly what he said. Briefly, however, it amounted to this—that he loved me and wanted to marry me.

About that time he wrote in his diary :

" *September 12, 1862.*—I did not believe I could ever be as much in love as I am. I'll go mad, I'll kill myself, if this goes on much longer. They had a party. She was fascinating in every respect.

" *September 13, 1862.*—I'll tell her everything first thing to-morrow morning—or else shoot myself. It's past 3 a.m. I have written her a letter which I'll hand to her to-morrow—or, rather, to-day, the 14th. God, how afraid I am to die ! Such great happiness is incredible ! Good God, help me ! "

The 15th went past, and on Saturday, September 16, the cadets arrived—Sasha and his pals. We had tea in the dining-room, and were busy feeding the starving cadets. Lev Nikolaevich had spent the whole day with us ; and at last choosing a moment when no one was watching, he called me into my mother's room, which was empty at the time.

" I wanted to speak to you," he said, " but I couldn't do it. Here is a letter which I have now been carrying in my pocket for several days. Read it. I shall wait here for your answer."

THE PROPOSAL

I seized the letter and rushed downstairs into the girls' room, which the three of us shared. Here is the letter :

" Sophie Andreyevna, it is becoming unbearable. For three weeks I've been saying to myself : ' I shall tell her now,' and yet I continue to go away with the same feeling of sadness, regret, terror, and happiness in my heart. Every night I go over the past and curse myself for not having spoken to you, and wonder what I would have said if I *had* spoken. I am taking this letter with me, in order to hand it to you should my courage fail me again. Your family have the false notion, I believe, that I am in love with Lisa. This is quite wrong. Your story has clung to my mind because, after reading it, I have come to the conclusion that 'Prince Dublitsky' has no right to think of happiness, that your poetic view of love is different . . . that I am not jealous, and must not be jealous, of the man you will love. I thought I could love you all like children. I wrote at Ivitsy, 'Your presence reminds me too vividly of my old age'—*your* presence in particular. But then, as now, I was lying to myself. At Ivitsy I might still have been able to break away and to return to my hermitage, back to my solitary work and my absorbing labours. Now I can't do anything; I feel I have created a disturbance in your home, and that your friendship for me, as a good, honourable man, has also been spoiled. I dare not leave, and I dare not stay. You are a candid, honest girl; with your hand on your heart, and without hurrying (for God's sake, don't hurry!), tell me what to do. I would have laughed myself sick a month ago if I had been told that I would suffer, suffer joyfully, as I have been doing for this past month. Tell me, with all the candour that is yours: Will you be my wife? If you can say *yes*, *boldly*, with all your heart, then *say it*; but if you have the faintest shadow of doubt, say *no*. For heaven's sake, think it over carefully. I am terrified to think of a *no*, but I am prepared for it and will be strong enough to bear it. But it will be terrible if I am not loved by my wife as much as I love you ! "

I didn't read the letter carefully, I merely skipped over it till I reached the words, " Will you be my wife ? " I was going to return upstairs and say yes to Lev Nikolaevich, when I ran into Lisa, who asked me : " Well ? "

" Le comte m'a fait la proposition," I answered quickly. Mother came in then, and realised at once what had happened. She took me firmly by the shoulders and, turning my face to the door, she said, " Go and give him your answer."

I flew up the stairs, as light as a feather, and, rushing past the dining-room and drawing-room, I flew into my mother's bedroom. Lev Nikolaevich stood in the corner, leaning against the wall, waiting for me. I went up to him, and he took me by both hands.

" Well ? " he asked.

" Of course—yes," I replied.

A few minutes later everybody in the house knew what had happened, and began to congratulate us.

THE NAME-DAY : THE BRIDE

The next day, September 17, was Mother's name-day, as well as mine. All our Moscow relations and friends came to congratulate us, and everybody was told of our engagement. When the old university professor, who taught us French, heard that it was I, and not my elder sister, who had become engaged to Lev Nikolaevich, he said naïvely :

" C'est dommage que cela ne fût Mlle. Lise ; elle a si bien étudié."

Little Katya Obolensky, however, embraced me joyfully, saying :

" I am so glad you are getting married to such a fine man and writer."

My engagement lasted for only a week—from September 16 to September 23. During that time I was taken round shops, where, with a feeling of complete indifference, I tried on dresses, linen, hats, and bonnets. Lev Nikolaevich kept coming daily, and once brought me his diaries to read. These diaries, which he made me read, before our wedding, out of an excessive sense of duty, upset me very much. He shouldn't have done it ; it made me cry as I looked into his past.

One evening, I remember, Mother and my sisters went to the theatre to see Alridge, the famous tragedian, act Othello. Mother sent a carriage for us, so that we, too, might go to the show. I was slightly afraid of Lev Nikolaevich then—afraid that he would soon grow disappointed in such a silly, insignificant little girl as me. I kept silent nearly all the way.

Once he arrived in the middle of the day and found me in the drawing-room with my friend, Olga Z., who, sitting at the window, was weeping bitterly.

Lev Nikolaevich was much surprised.

" It looks as if you were burying her," he said.

" If you take her away," she said in French, unable to control her tears, " it'll be the end, and we shall have lost her for ever."

That week passed like a bad dream. To many people my wedding was a cause for sorrow, and Lev Nikolaevich was in a hurry to get through with it. But Mother said that at least a part of my trousseau ought to be made before the wedding.

" Surely she's got enough clothes," said Lev Nikolaevich, " she's always perfectly well dressed."

In the end they managed to get some of the trousseau done, particularly the wedding dress, and the wedding was announced for September 23 at 7 p.m. at the Palace Church. Our house was in a state of turmoil, but Lev Nikolaevich, too, had plenty to worry about. He bought a splendid *dormeuse*, ordered a photograph of my family, and gave me a diamond brooch. He also had his own photo taken, which I had asked him to fit into the gold bracelet that father had given me. Moreover, a certain Mr. Stellovsky,[16] to whom he sold the copyright of his books, was giving him a lot of worry and annoyance. But neither the dresses nor the presents gave me much pleasure ; I was taken up with other things. I kept thinking of my love for Lev Nikolaevich and of my fear of losing his. This fear has lived in my heart throughout my life, although, thank the Lord, we never stopped loving each other during all the forty-eight years we have been together.

In discussing our future, Lev Nikolaevich asked me where I would like to live after my wedding—whether I would like to stay for some time with my people in Moscow, or go abroad, or go straight to Yasnaya Polyana. I chose Yasnaya Polyana, for I wanted to start our married life straightaway *at home*. This apparently pleased him very much.

THE WEDDING DAY

At last the wedding day came. I didn't see Lev Nikolaevich all that day. He only dropped in for a minute, and as we sat down on the ready-packed luggage, he began to torture me with questions and doubts about my love for him. It even occurred to me that he might want to run away, having suddenly got frightened at the last moment. I began to weep. Mother came in and pounced on Lev Nikolaevich. "You've chosen a fine time for upsetting her," she said ; "to-day is her wedding day, and it's all very tiring, especially with the long journey in front of her ; and there she is now, crying." This, evidently, made Lev Nikolaevich feel uncomfortable. He soon went away and had dinner with Vasili Stepanovich and Praskovya Feodorovna Perfilyev, who were to be his "wedding father" and "wedding mother." They gave him their blessing and took him to the church. Timiryazev was his best man, as his brother, Sergei Nikolaevich Tolstoy[11] had gone to Yasnaya Polyana to make preparations for our reception. He was to meet us there.

The only near relation of his who attended the wedding was his aunt, Pelageya Ilyinishna Yushkov. She drove to the church in my carriage, with me and little Volodya, who carried the ikon.

After six, my sisters and girl friends began to dress me. I asked them not to call for a hairdresser, and did my hair myself, while the girls helped me to pin on the flowers and the long tulle veil. The dress was tulle, too, as the fashion of the time demanded ; very open in front and with frills at the sleeves. The whole thing was so thin and airy, and seemed to envelop me like a cloud. My slender, girlish arms and hands looked bony and pitiful. At last I was ready, and we began to wait for the best man, who would come to announce that the bridegroom was in the church. But an hour passed, and still no one had arrived. The thought shot through my head that he had run away ; he had behaved so strangely in the morning. Suddenly, instead of the best man, Lev Nikolaevich's valet, the squint-eyed little Alexey Stepanovich, came rushing along, in a state of great excitement, and asked us to hurry up and open the portmanteau and take out a clean shirt. In the heat of excitement, when they were packing up the luggage, they had forgotten to leave out a shirt for the wedding ! They had sent someone round to buy one, but it was Sunday and all the shops were closed. Before everything was right, another hour or so elapsed. But at last the best man arrived announcing that the bridegroom was at the church. Then there was no end to the tears and sobs of all the women around me, and all this upset me completely.

" What'll we do without our little countess," my old nurse whimpered. She had always called me that, probably in memory of my grandmother, Countess Sophie Zavadovsky, after whom I was named.

" I'll die of loneliness when you are gone," Tanya kept on repeating.

Petya, my little brother, kept looking at me wistfully with his large black eyes. Mother seemed to avoid me, and kept rushing around, preparing for the reception. My heart was heavy at the thought of leaving them all.

Father was unwell; I went to his study to say good-bye to him, and he was kind to me and seemed deeply moved. Then they got the bread and salt ready, and Mother took down the ikon of St. Sophie, and, with her brother Michael Alexandrovich Islenyev[18] standing at her side, she blessed me with it.

We drove in solemn silence to the church, which wasn't a stone's-throw away from our house. I was weeping all the way. The winter garden and the Church of the Birth of the Holy Virgin were splendidly lit up. Lev Nikolaevich met me in the palace garden, and, taking me by the hand, led me to the altar. The palace choir were singing, the service was conducted by two priests, and everything was very elegant and magnificent. All the guests had already assembled in the church, and there were also many strangers, mostly servants, from the palace. The public kept passing remarks about my extreme youth and the redness of my eyes.

The marriage ceremony has been splendidly described in *Anna Karenina*. In his account of Levin's and Kitty's wedding, Lev Nikolaevich has not only given a vivid and brilliant picture of the ceremony, but has also described the whole psychological process in the bridegroom's mind. As for myself, I had lived through so much excitement during the last few days that, standing at the altar, I felt and experienced absolutely nothing. It seemed to me that something obvious, natural, and inevitable was happening—nothing more. I felt that all this *had* to be, and that it was useless to question it.

My brother Sasha and his friend P., then an officer of the Guards, were my best men.

When the ceremony was over, everybody rushed to congratulate us, and then the two of us drove home together. He was very affectionate, and, evidently, happy. . . . At home at the Kremlin, the usual wedding reception had been prepared—champagne, fruit, sweets, etc. There were few guests—only our relations and some of our most intimate friends.

I was taken away to change into my travelling dress. Barbara, our aged maid, whom Dr. Anke, an old friend of my father's, had jokingly named the "Oyster," and whom I was taking with me, was busy helping Lev Nikolaevich's valet to pack up the last things and to put the finishing touches to the luggage.

THE DEPARTURE

Six mail horses were harnessed into the new *dormeuse* which Lev Nikolaevich had just bought, the black shining trunks were strapped to the top of the carriage, and Lev Nikolaevich was in a hurry to get away. A heavy, painful feeling began to choke me. I suddenly realised clearly for the first time that I was breaking away *for ever* from my family and all whom I had loved all my life. But I tried to suppress my tears and my sorrow. I began to say good-bye. It was terrible ! When I said good-bye to my sick father, I burst out crying. Kissing Lisa good-bye, I looked closely into her eyes ; she, also, was weeping. Tanya cried loudly, like a child, and so did Petya, who, as he later explained, had taken too much champagne to drown his sorrow ; so they took him off to bed. I then went downstairs and blessed with the sign of the cross little Vyacheslav, who was fast asleep ; I said good-bye to my nurse, Vera Ivanovna, who, throwing her arms round me, kissed me effusively. Stepanida Trifonovna, a reserved little thing who had lived with us for thirty-five years, said courteously that she wished me much happiness.

But finally the last moment arrived which I had specially reserved for my mother. Just before taking my place in the carriage, I threw myself round her neck. We both sobbed. And in those sobs was expressed our mutual gratitude for all the love and kindness we had given each other, the forgiveness for all the involuntary pain we had caused each other, my sorrow at being separated from my beloved mother, and her motherly wish that I should be happy.

When at last I wrenched myself away, and, without looking round, took my seat in the carriage, she let out a piercing cry which I remembered for the rest of my life. I could never forget that cry, which seemed to have been torn straight from my mother's heart.

The autumn rain was pouring down, and the puddles reflected the dim lights of the street lanterns. The horses were growing impatient, and the ones in front, with the rider, kept straining at the reins. Lev Nikolaevich shut the carriage door with a bang. Alexey Stepanovich and the "Oyster" took their seats at the back. The horses' feet began to splash through the puddles, and so we drove away. I sat huddled up in my corner, tired and heart-broken, and kept on weeping. Lev Nikolaevich seemed surprised and dismayed. He had never had a real family—neither father nor mother ; he was brought up without them ; and, in any case, being a man, he could not have understood my feelings. He remarked that I evidently did not love him very much if leaving my family meant such great sorrow to me. He did not realise then that if I was capable of so much love for my family, I would later on transfer it to him and to our children ; which, indeed, was what happened.

When we got out of Moscow, it became very dark and weird. I had never travelled anywhere in autumn or winter before. The darkness and the absence of lanterns depressed me terribly. We hardly spoke a word until we reached Birulevo, the first stop. Lev Nikolaevich, I remember, was particularly gentle with me.

At Birulevo a titled honeymoon couple, arriving in a new *dormeuse* driven by six horses, naturally created a sensation. We were given a state apartment, very large and unfriendly, with nothing but a few pieces of red damask furniture in it. They brought in the samovar and put on the tea. I crouched in a corner of a sofa and sat there silently, like one condemned to death.

" Well, show that you are the mistress here," said Lev Nikolaevich. " Come on, pour out the tea."*

I obeyed and we had tea, but I still felt very much embarrassed, as if afraid of something. I didn't once dare call him *thou*, and avoided using any pronoun at all, and for a long time afterwards I still called him *you*.

OUR ARRIVAL AT YASNAYA POLYANA

It took a little under twenty-four hours to travel from Moscow to Yasnaya Polyana, and, much to my

* Here, for the first time, Tolstoy addresses her in the second person singular.

joy, we reached my new home in the evening of the next day. It was a strange feeling. I was *at home*, and where ? In Yasnaya Polyana.

The first thing I saw as I went up the steps of the house where I was destined to live for fifty years was Aunt Tatiana Alexandrovna, holding up the ikon of the Holy Virgin, and, next to her, Sergei Nikolaevich, my brother-in-law, with the bread and salt. I bowed down to the ground, and, making the sign of the cross, I kissed the ikon and Aunt Tatiana. L. N. did likewise. Then we went to her room, where we found Nathalie Petrovna. With that day my life in Yasnaya Polyana began, and I hardly ever left the place during the first eighteen years of our marriage.

The next day Lev Nikolaevich wrote in his diary :

> " *September 25, 1862.*—Incredible happiness ! I can't believe that this can last as long as life ! "

VARIOUS ENTRIES FOR FUTURE REFERENCE (1870–1881)

VARIOUS ENTRIES FOR FUTURE REFERENCE (1870-1881)

YASNAYA POLYANA,
February 14, 1870.

As I was reading Pushkin's life the other day, it occurred to me that I might render a service to posterity by recording, not so much Lyova's everyday life, as his mental activities, so far as I was able to watch them. I had often thought of it before, but I had had very little time for it.

This is a good time to begin. *War and Peace* is completed, and nothing else very important has yet been begun. He spent all last summer reading and studying philosophy : he spoke very highly of Schopenhauer, but thought Hegel a bagful of empty phrases. He spent much time on painful reflection, and often said that his brain was aching with all the strain, that he was of no further use, that it was time to die, etc. Later on, however, these gloomy moods passed. He began to read Russian folk-tales and *byliny*.* This gave him the idea of writing and compiling children's books for four stages, the first one beginning with the alphabet.[11] The tales and *byliny* delighted him. He even meant to use the Danila epic as the subject for a play. Other characters, such as Ilya Murometz, Alyosha Popovich, etc., fascinated him so much that he thought of writing a novel on the subject of some of these old Russian heroes. He

* Folk epics.

particularly liked Ilya Murometz, and meant to describe him in his novel as an educated and very intelligent man of peasant origin who had studied at a university. I can't exactly describe the character as he outlined him to me, but I know that it was very finely done. After reading folk-tales and *byliny*, he started reading an immense number of plays. He read Molière, Shakespeare, and Pushkin's *Boris Godunov*, which he dislikes ; and now he intends to write a comedy. He even began to tell me of a rather silly subject, but I don't really consider that as part of his serious work. He himself said to me the other day : "No, after one has tried the epic manner" (*War and Peace*), "it is very difficult to change over to drama." But I can see that the idea of writing a comedy appeals to him, and that he is anxious to try his hand at drama.

February 5.

Last night Lyova talked of Shakespeare at great length, and praised him highly : he sees in Shakespeare an immense dramatic talent.* He considered Goethe very plastic, elegant, and æsthetic, but denied him dramatic talent. He said he had often meant to discuss the matter with Fet,[10] who admired Goethe immensely. Lyova added that Goethe became truly great only when he began to argue and philosophise. This morning L. called me into his study and talked a great deal about Russian history and some of its characters. I found him reading Ustryalov's *History of Peter the Great.*

* (A later entry). His praise of Shakespeare was always of short duration. Fundamentally, he disliked him, and often said : "But I'm telling you this as a secret."

He is much interested in the characters of Peter and Menshikov.

He considers Menshikov a strong Russian character of typical peasant origin. Peter the Great, he said, was the tool of his age, and the task of bringing Russia and Europe together, which fate had imposed upon him, must have been a painful one. He is looking in history for a dramatic subject, and takes notes on anything he thinks suitable. To-day he wrote down the story of Mirovich,[11] who had wanted to release Prince Ioann Antonovich from the Fortress. Yesterday he said that he had given up thinking of a comedy and was looking for a subject for a serious drama. He repeated several times: "What a lot of work ahead!"

We have just been out skating. He tries hard to do all the tricks on one and then on both legs, such as running backwards, doing circles, etc. It amuses him like a little boy.

February 24, 1870.

After much hesitation, L. has at last settled down to work to-day. Yesterday he said that, on thinking it over carefully, he had come to the conclusion that it was the epic and not the dramatic manner that appealed to him most.

He had been to see Fet lately, who had told him that his talent wasn't a dramatic one, and I believe he has now given up thinking of his comedy and drama.

This morning he covered a large sheet with his close writing. The action starts in a monastery with a large crowd of people, who include all the main characters of the book.

Last night he said that he had conceived the character of a married woman of high rank but who had lost her balance. He said that he would try to make this woman pitiable and blameless, and that no sooner had he imagined her clearly than he also visualised all the other male and female characters of the story whom he had thought of before. "Now I can see everything clearly," he said. He intends making an estate manager of the educated peasant, whom he had thought out before.

"I am being accused of fatalism," he said, "and yet there is no more religious man than myself. Fatalism is an excuse for doing evil, while I believe in God and in the saying of the Gospel that even the very hairs of your head are all numbered, and that everything is predestined." We get neither papers nor magazines. L. says he doesn't want to read criticism. "Pushkin was always annoyed at critics; it is better not to read them." *The Dawn*, in which Strakhov praises L. up to the skies, is being sent us free of charge. L. is much pleased with Strakhov's articles. Ries also sends us a German paper, and beyond this and the *Revue des Deux Mondes*, to which we subscribe, we see nothing.

December 9, 1870.

I believe that he has at last begun to write in earnest to-day. I can hardly say how worried he was during his period of inaction. He had two ideas, one about a man's travels in Russia, the other about the educated peasant. At the beginning of the story which he read to me, there is again the idea of a proud and extraordinarily brilliant man who wants to teach others, and to be of general use, but who, after travelling about Russia and meeting several simple and genuinely useful people, finally comes to the conclusion that his idea of usefulness is wrong ; and so he takes a calm and humble view of life which, he knows, must ultimately end in death. At least, that's the way I understood it from what L. told me.

Just now he is in the drawing-room with a theological student who is giving him his first Greek lesson. He suddenly took a fancy to learning Greek.

The inactivity of these last months (though I would call it mental rest) has been getting on his nerves. He said he was ashamed of his idleness, not only because of me, but because of what other people might think. At times he believed that his inspiration was returning to him, and it made him happy.

He sometimes imagines (but only when he is away from his home), that he will go insane, and his fear of madness is so intense that I am terrified whenever he speaks of it.

He came back from Moscow two days ago. He brought us back some dolls, Christmas-tree decorations, a length of cloth, etc., and kept on repeating : "What a joy to be at home with one's children ! What a delight they are ! " He tutors Serezha[**] in mathematics, and sometimes loses his temper. But he tells Serezha always to check him if he gets too angry.

March 27, 1871.

He has been studying Greek with great perseverance ever since December, and pores over it by day and night. Nothing seems to give him greater joy than to learn some new Greek word or idiom. He used to read Xenophon, but has now taken up Plato, the *Odyssey* and the *Iliad*, which he admires immensely. He likes me to listen to his verbal translation, which he gets me to compare with Gnedich's and correct him when he is wrong. He thinks Gnedich a very fine and conscientious translator. To judge from what other Greek students have learned at school, and even at the university, his progress seems quite unusually great. In comparing his translation with Gnedich's I hardly ever find more than one or two mistakes to a page.

He wants to get back to writing, and often says so. He keeps thinking, above all, of a book that would be as pure, as elegant, and as devoid of superfluous matter as the art and literature of the ancient Greeks. I can't very well explain it, but I seem to understand the kind of book he means. He says that " it is not difficult to write things, but very difficult *not* to write them " ; that is to say, to avoid writing empty phrases—an art that very few have mastered.

He is hoping to write a book on ancient Russian life. He reads the *Chetyi-Minei* and the lives of the saints, which, he says, represent the real poetry of the Russian people. His health is poor, and he has been unwell all winter. The pain in his knee has been terrible, and he has often had a temperature, largely due, as he himself admits, to the strain of learning Greek ; and now he also has a dry, hacking cough, which he refuses to notice and grows angry each time I mention it. " That isn't a cough," he always says, and that upsets me more than anything else.

December 16, 1873.

I haven't kept to my resolution of recording the life and labours of L. Since I last wrote he has compiled four books for children, proudly working on them with the firm conviction that the work is good and useful. His A B C book is a terrible failure, and this, especially at first, grieved and annoyed him considerably.[11] Fortunately, however, that did not keep him from working. Yesterday he said : " If my novel had been as great a failure, I would readily have believed that it was poor. But I am quite convinced that my A B C is unusually good, and that people have simply failed to understand its purpose."

He is now busy reading documents on the times of Peter the Great. He has suddenly been seized with an unconscious desire to apply his mind to that particular period. I hardly noticed how it came over him. He writes down in little note-books anything that may be useful in describing the manners, habits, clothes, houses, and furniture of the period, particularly of the people who are not connected with the Tsar and the Court. In another book he notes down anything that occurs to him about the story, the characters, the poetic descriptions, etc. It's the most detailed kind of work. He is so much interested in details that he came back yesterday from shooting at an unusually early hour in order to examine his materials and make sure whether in the days of Peter the Great they wore high collars or not with the short *kaftan*. L. believes that the high collars were worn only with long coats, especially among the common people. In the evening he read some memoirs on the customs and marriage rites in the days of Alexey

Mikhailovich.[26] Lyova spoke very highly of Ustryalov's history, which he regards as a very conscientious piece of work.

January 31, 1873.

He continues to read historical material, and the characters reveal themselves to him one after the other.

He has written about ten different openings, but is still dissatisfied. Yesterday he said : " The machine is ready, the problem is to get it to start."

March 19, 1873.

Last night L. suddenly said to me : " I have written a sheet and a half, and I believe it's good." I didn't take much notice of these words, thinking they referred to still another attempt to describe the age of Peter the Great. But later I found that he had begun to write a modern novel of family life. It is strange he should have started it so suddenly.

Serezha has been bothering me to let him have something that he could read aloud to his old aunt. I gave him Pushkin's *Stories of Belkin*. But Aunt had already gone to sleep, and I, being too lazy to take the book back to the library, left it lying on the drawing-room window. The next morning, while he was having coffee, L. picked it up, and, glancing through it, went into raptures of praise. He found some critical notes at the beginning of the volume (it was Annenkov's edition) and said : " I have learned, and am still learning, so much from Pushkin ! Pushkin is my father and my teacher." He then read aloud some passages about the past, how the squires of that time lived and went about the country, and he thought that all this explained many of the problems that had puzzled him about the life of the gentry in the days of Peter the Great. In the evening he read some other fragments and, still under the influence of Pushkin, began to write. To-day he went on with it, and said that he was satisfied with his work.

He has just gone out with his two sons, Feodor Feodorovich (their tutor) and Uncle Kostya, to have a look at the fox. This fox is seen at the bridge near our house every day. The weather is gloriously clear. In the day-time the sun is dazzling, and at night the stars and the sharp sickle of the moon sparkle brilliantly.

October 4, 1873.

L. began *Anna Karenina* last spring, and outlined its whole plan at the same time. During the entire summer, which we spent in the Samara region, L. did no writing, but now he is busy once again correcting, polishing, and going on with the novel. Kramskoy[27] is painting two portraits of L., and this rather interferes with the work. But, on the other hand, they have daily talks and discussions on art.

Yesterday we drove to the Obolenskys at Shakhovskoye. L. was coughing, which worried me greatly. He went on further to shoot, while I returned home. (It is Tanya's[28] ninth birthday to-day.)

November 20, 1876.

L. N. has just been telling me how the ideas for his novel came to him :

" I was sitting alone in my study and looking at the

fine white silk embroidery on the sleeve of my dressing-gown. This made me wonder how people came to think of all this sewing and stitching and embroidery, and I realised that it represented a whole world of women's daily cares and interests ; that it must all be very fascinating and that it was no wonder that women went in for it. And my thoughts naturally turned to Anna Karenina, and in the end this bit of embroidery on my sleeve suggested a whole chapter to me. Anna is cut off from this joyful side of a woman's existence, for she is alone, abandoned by all women, and she has no one to talk to about a subject of such universal, everyday interest to women." All autumn he used to say : " My brain is asleep " ; but suddenly, about a week ago, something within him seemed to have burst forth into blossom : he started to work cheerfully and is thoroughly satisfied with his energy and work. This morning, before even taking his coffee, he sat down to write and went on for more than an hour, and altered the chapter on Alexander Alexandrovich's relation to Lydia Ivanovna, and the one on Anna's arrival in St. Petersburg.

November 21, 1876.

He came up to me and said : " It's so dull writing this." " Writing what ? " I asked. " Well, I have said that Vronsky and Anna were staying at the same room at the hotel, and that's impossible. On their arrival in Petersburg they simply must take rooms on different floors. As a result, it is going to be very difficult to arrange all the scenes with the persons who call to see them. The whole thing will have to be changed."

March 3, 1877.

L. N. went up to his table yesterday, and, pointing at the manuscript, said : " I wish I could have this finished soon (i.e. *Anna Karenina*), so that I could start on something new. My idea is perfectly clear now. A work can only be good if one loves its fundamental, central idea. Thus, in *Anna Karenina*, I love the idea of the *family*, in *War and Peace*, in view of the war of 1812, the idea of the *people* ; the central idea of my new book will be the *power of expansion* of the Russian people." He sees an expression of this in the constant migration of Russians to new lands in the south-east, in Southern Siberia, in the Belaya River region, in Turkestan," etc.

A great deal is heard about all this migration nowadays. We spent last summer in the Samara region, and the two of us drove to a Cossack settlement some fifteen miles from our Samara farm. On the way we met a long procession of carts with several families, including children and old men, all very happy. We stopped and asked where they were going. " We are coming from Voronezh and are going to new parts. Some of our folks have settled in the Amur region and have written to us from there, and now we are going there too."

Lev Nikolaevich was much interested and excited at this. Just now, at the railway station, he was told of another case of how a hundred Tambov peasants migrated to Siberia on their own initiative. When they reached the steppe near the Irtysh River, they were told that this land belonged to some Kirghiz tribes and that they would not be allowed to settle there. So they went on a little further. There, too, they weren't allowed to stay, and for the same reason. By this time they had very little money and food left. So they sowed wheat on that land, and, after gathering and threshing it, they went on. They did the same the following year, and so on, until they at last reached the Chinese border. There they found on the banks of two little rivers some land that had been abandoned by the Manchurians. Here the Tambov peasants settled down, and named the two rivers after the two little rivers at home. And so, although the land originally belonged to China, it became Russian soil, conquered not with blood and war, but by the agricultural strength of the Russian *mujik*. Occasionally the Manchurians attack them, but the Russians have built a fort and are able to protect themselves.

Here is the idea for the future book as I understand it, and in the meantime new facts and characters accumulate around it, though some of these are still rather vague, even in his mind.[10]

Returning to-day from his morning walk, L. N. said : " I am so happy ! " " What is making you happy ? " I asked. " First of all, you, and, secondly, my religion. I have not been converted to the ' new Christianity ' by either Bobrinsky[11] or Alexandra Andreyevna Tolstoy ; but Levitsky (who was here yesterday) and Doctor Zakharyin, the materialist, have greatly impressed me. Zakharyin has converted me by his earnest desire to be religious, and Levitsky by his stories of Russian history, which he treats from an original and excellent new angle—the religious one."

The point of Levitsky's historical stories is that in the

old days the Russians were not Christians, but lived merely for their own selfish needs, and God punished them for it ; later on, however, they became Christians and began to live for their souls. L. N. was deeply moved at reading those stories, and to-day he said that he couldn't much longer endure the terrible religious crisis which had been torturing him for the past two years, and that he hoped that the time was near when he would become a thoroughly religious man, and not . . . (I was interrupted at this point and don't remember what I meant to say.)

August 25, 1877.

L. N. has gone to Moscow in search of a tutor for the children. The spirit of religion is taking a firmer hold on him every day. He now says his prayers daily, as he did in his childhood, and goes to midday Mass on Sundays, where all the peasants crowd round asking him about the war ; he eats lenten food on Wednesdays and Fridays ; he often speaks of the spirit of humility, and half-jokingly stops the others if they condemn anyone. He visited the Optina Monastery on July 26, and greatly praised the mode of life, the wisdom, and the culture of the monks there.

Yesterday he said : " The valve of my mind has been opened at last, only it gives me a headache." He is much perturbed by our reverses in the Turkish War and by the internal affairs of Russia, and he spent all morning yesterday writing on the subject. In the evening he said that the best way of expressing his ideas would be to write a letter to the Tsar. Let him write it ; but it is a dangerous thing to do, and it must not be sent off.

September 12, 1877.

L. N. said : " I can't write anything while the war" is going on ; one has the same feeling when there's a fire in the town ; the excitement is so great that you can't give your attention to anything else." He has gone out shooting with his wolf-hounds to-day, and afterwards will go on to Nikolskoye to see about the farm work.

October 25, 1877

L. N. has gone out shooting now with his hounds, but in the morning he was telling me how the thoughts were beginning to collect in his mind for his new book. I can't see quite clearly yet what exactly he is proposing to write and I don't believe he has thought it out very clearly himself. But, so far as I could make out, the main theme is the people and their strength, which reveals itself exclusively in agriculture. To-day he said to me : " I like that proverb very much which I read yesterday : ' One son is no son, two sons are half a son, three sons are a son.' That will be the motto at the beginning. I'll have an old man in the story with three sons. One is a soldier ; the next is nothing special, living at home ; the third, the old man's favourite, learns to read and write, and greatly hurts his father by turning away from the peasant life. Here is the tragedy in the mind of a wealthy peasant ; it is something to start with." After that the clever son comes into touch with some people of the educated class, and this leads to a series of events. In the second part, L. N.

said, there will be a settler, a Russian Robinson Crusoe, who settles on new land in the Samara steppes and starts an entirely new life, made up of only the most indispensable factors of existence.

" I find the description of peasant life extremely interesting, but difficult ; I feel more at home describing our own life," said L. N.

Anna Karenina is being printed, and will soon appear in a separate edition. L. N. said to-day : " In my new book the main idea will be revealed as clearly as in *Anna Karenina*." But what is this new central idea ?

December 26, 1877.

At three in the morning on December 6 our son Andrey was born. This seems to have liberated L. N.'s mind from certain mental chains, and a week ago he began to write some new philosophic-religious work in a large bound volume. I haven't read it yet, but to-day he said to his brother Stepa : " The thing I am writing in the large book aims at showing the absolute necessity for religion."

I like the argument in favour of Christianity with which he opposes the arguments of the Socialists and Communists that the social laws are deeper than the Christian laws, and that is why I am going to record it. It is this : " If there had been no Christian laws, which for centuries have been the basis of our social life, there would have been no laws of morality or honour, nor would the people have desired equality, goodness, and a fairer distribution of wealth."

L. N.'s mood undergoes great changes as time goes on. After a long struggle between irreligiousness and the desire for religion, he has suddenly calmed down with the coming of autumn. He has begun to fast and pray and go to church. When he is asked why he has chosen these particular rites, he replies : " I shall try to conform to all the laws of the Church, but, meantime, I am following as many as I can." He keeps on asking us : " Will you go to Confession ? " " Yes." "The priest will ask you if you eat lenten food." " He will." " Well, you must either eat it or else lie to him."

L. N.'s character is changing more and more. Although he has always been very modest and simple in his habits and requirements, he is becoming even more modest, meeker, and more tolerant. This great struggle for moral self-perfection, which began in his early youth, must surely be crowned with success.

January 8, 1878.

" Something is happening to me now which reminds me of the time when I wrote *War and Peace*," said L. N. to-day, with a faint smile which seemed half-happy and half-doubtful of the words he uttered. " Then, too, as I was going to write about the return of a Decembrist from Siberia, I first went back to the period of the revolt, and then to the childhood and youth of the Decembrists, and so I grew interested in the war of 1812 ; but, as this war was connected with the war of 1805, I ultimately began my book with that period." L. N. is at present greatly interested in the reign of Nicholas I, and, above all, in the Turkish war of 1829. He has started studying that period, and, while doing so, he has become interested in the accession of Nicholas I and the December revolt.

He also said to me : " All this is going to take place on Olympus, with Nicholas I and the aristocracy as Jupiter with his gods, while somewhere in Irkutsk and Samara, the peasants continue their migration. One of the December rioters falls among them, and thus ' the simple life ' comes in contact with the life of the nobility." He went on to say that, just as embroidery requires a canvas, so every story needs a background, and that in his new book this background would be made up of his religious ideas. " How is that ? " I inquired. " If I knew how," he said, " I wouldn't need to think of it any more." But later on he added : " The thing to do is simply to understand and to describe the December riot, without condemning anybody—either Nicholas I or the conspirators."

March 1, 1878.

L. N. is busy all the time, reading up the reign of Nicholas I, and he is particularly interested in the history of the Decembrists. He has been in Moscow and has brought back a large pile of books, and is often moved to tears when he reads the memoirs of the time. He has gone to Sergievskoye to-day to see about the help which is being organised for the soldiers' families.

December 18, 1879.

He is writing about religion, and the disagreement between the Church and Christianity. He reads all day long, and eats lenten food on Wednesdays and Fridays ; Zakharyin won't allow him to fast throughout the whole of Lent because of his headaches, which are probably due to his digestion. All his conversation is full of the teaching of Christ.

His frame of mind is peaceful, meditative, and solemn. He has put aside the Decembrists and all his former labours, although he still says sometimes : " If I ever write anything again, I shall write something quite different. All I have written so far has been mere exercise."

January 31, 1881.

Yuryev, the editor of the *Russkaya Mysl* has been here. When Lev Nikolaevich, taking his glass of tea with him, retired to work in his study from lunch till dinner (12 to 5) and I remained alone in the room with Yuryev, the latter started asking me why L. N. had given up writing *The Decembrists.* I had never before considered the question very carefully, but now I began to think it over, and gave Yuryev a long account of what had happened. When I was finished, Yuryev said excitedly : " Your story is extremely valuable ; you must write it down."

And so I am now following his advice.

L. N. only works hard during the winter months. He had studied the historical materials and had sketched out some of the book, but had not done anything very important by the beginning of summer. In order to make full use of his time, he started going for long walks along the Kiev main road, which is one and a half miles from here, and where in the summer one meets large numbers of pilgrims coming from every corner of Russia and Siberia and going to Kiev, Voronezh, Troitza, and other holy places.

As L. N. considered that his Russian was neither good nor sufficiently complete, he made it his aim to study the language of the people during the summer months, and so he used to talk at great length to pilgrims, " holy men," and various passers-by, and would write down all the popular proverbs, words, and idioms which he heard them use. This work suddenly had an unexpected result.

Until about 1877 L. N. was more or less indifferent to religion. He was never an absolute unbeliever, but he did not have any very *definite* faith. This tortured him greatly—indeed, he wrote his religious confession at the beginning of his new work.

Having come into close contact with the people, with pilgrims, and with " holy men," he became deeply impressed by their strong, lucid, and unassailable faith. He grew terrified at his own lack of faith, and suddenly, with all his heart, he decided to follow the path of these people. He began to go to Mass, to eat lenten food, to pray, and to carry out all the commands of the Church. This went on for quite a long time.

But L. N. soon came to realise that the teaching of the Church was not the source of all the love, goodness, and patience that he had observed in the people ; he said that, having seen the *rays*, he had followed these to their source, and had found that this source of light was not the Church, but Christianity itself, as taught in the Gospels. He firmly denies any other influence. I have taken all this down from his own words.

He also said : " Christianity lives in the spirit and in the legends of the people, unconsciously but steadfastly."

Little by little L. N. realised to his horror the great disparity between the Church and Christianity. He saw that, hand-in-hand with the Government, the Church had built up a conspiracy against Christianity. The Church thanks God for the slaughter of men and rejoices in military victories, and yet the Old Testament says : " Thou shalt not kill," and the Gospel : " Love thy neighbour as thyself." The Church approves of the oath, while Christ spoke against it. The Church created ritual, with which people are told to save themselves, and has put a check on Christianity ; the doctrine of the kingdom of God on earth has been obscured by the fact that the people have been made to believe in complete salvation through such things as baptism, communion, and fasting.

This is L. N.'s central idea at present. He has begun to study the Gospel and to translate and interpret it. This work has now been going on for two years and he must be about half-way through it by now. He has become, as he says, " happy in the soul." He has seen what he calls *the light*. His whole view of life has been illuminated by it. As for his relation to people, he now says that he used to have a small circle of *his own intimate* people, but that now all the millions of mankind have become his brothers. Before he had *his own* wealth and estates, but now if a poor man asks for anything it must be given to him.

He sits down to his work every day surrounded with books, and works on till dinner-time. He is in much poorer health, and suffers from headaches. He has grown thin during the past winter and his hair is turning grey.

It seems to me that he is not as happy as I should like him to be, but he has become gentle, thoughtful, and tense. His cheerful, happy moods of the past, which we all loved so much, hardly ever come to him now. This must be due to overwork and excessive strain. It was all so different in the days when he was writing his chapters on the ball and hunting in *War and Peace* ; he was so joyful and excited then, as though he himself were taking part in those entertainments. The calm serenity of his own soul is obvious, but thoughts of the suffering and the poverty of men—the prisoners in jail, all the hatred, oppression, and injustice in the world—all have a fearful effect on his impressionable soul and actually seem to be wearing him away.

WHY ANNA KARENINA WAS CALLED "ANNA," AND WHAT SUGGESTED TO TOLSTOY THE IDEA OF HER SUICIDE

We have a neighbour called A. N. Bibikov, a man of about fifty, who is neither rich nor very educated. A distant relative of his late wife was staying in his house, a woman of about thirty-five, who took care of the household and was his mistress. One day Bibikov got a new governess, a beautiful German woman, for his son and nephew. Before very long he fell in love, and proposed to her. His former mistress, whose name was *Anna* Stepanovna, went to Tula for the day, as if to visit her mother, but returned with a bundle of clothes to Yasenki, the nearest railway station, and there threw herself under a goods train. A post-mortem was held, which Lev Nikolaevich attended. He saw her there, lying in the Yasenka barrack, with her skull dissected and her naked body terribly mangled. The effect on his mind was terrible. Anna Stepanovna was a tall, heavily built woman, with a Russian character and Russian features, dark hair and grey eyes, and, though not beautiful, a very pleasant woman.

THE QUARREL BETWEEN TOLSTOY AND TURGENEV

The relations between Lev Nikolaevich and Turgenev were most friendly during the early stages of the former's literary career in St. Petersburg. Turgenev recognised his talent, and wrote some very complimentary letters on the subject to Maria Nikolaevna, L. N.'s sister. They often met, and were evidently great friends, although Turgenev was ten years older and did not like to find a literary rival in the younger man.

One day Turgenev and Tolstoy met at Fet's house, in the Mtsensk district, in the province of Orel. The conversation turned to charity, and Turgenev said that his daughter, who had been educated abroad, did much good in helping the poor.

L. N. said that he did not approve of the English type of charity, which consisted in choosing *one's own poor*, and in handing out to them, at stated periods, a certain minute fraction of one's own income. He said that real charity could only come spontaneously, from the heart.

To which Turgenev replied : " Do you mean, then, that I am bringing up my daughter badly ? " L. N. replied that he only meant what he said, and that he had expressed his thoughts without intending to be personal. Turgenev grew angry at this, and suddenly said : " If you go on talking like that, I'll punch you in the face."

L. N. got up and drove off to Boguslov, a station situated half-way between our estate, Nikolskoye, and Fet's. From there he sent for his gun and some cartridges, and at the same time addressed a letter to Turgenev challenging him to a duel.

In that letter he told Turgenev that he did not want any of those vulgar literary duels which began with pistols and ended with a bottle of champagne, but that he meant a real duel, and asked Turgenev to meet him with his guns outside the Boguslov forest.

L. N. did not sleep all night waiting for him. In the morning a letter came from Turgenev in which he explained that he could not agree to Tolstoy's demand, and that he wanted a regular duel conducted on the recognised lines. To this L. N. replied : " You are afraid of me. I despise you and will not have anything more to do with you."

A long time after that Tolstoy was living in Moscow when one of those wonderful moods came over him, one of those sudden moods of goodness and love and humility. In such a state of mind the thought of having an enemy was unbearable to him. He therefore wrote a letter to Turgenev, in which he said : " Forgive me if I have offended you ; it makes me unbearably sad to think that I may have an enemy." The letter was sent to Davydov, a bookseller with whom Turgenev had dealings. But before it reached Turgenev the latter had already sent L. N. the following reproachful letter from Paris :

" You are telling everybody that I am a coward and that I refused to fight with you. I now demand satisfaction, and shall fight you on my return to Russia "—which, I believe, was to be about eight months later.

Lev Nikolaevich replied that it was ridiculous to challenge a man to a duel eight months in advance, that he treated the challenge with contempt, and that, in case Turgenev felt the necessity of white-washing himself in public, he (Tolstoy) was sending him another letter which he could show to anyone he liked. In this letter Tolstoy wrote : " You said you would punch me in the face, and yet I refused to fight you."

This letter was meant to imply that, if Turgenev had no personal sense of honour, but merely a sense of dignity in relation to the world at large, he could by all means use the letter, but that L. N. was above such things and treated the opinion of the world with contempt. Turgenev once more showed the weakness of his character by replying that he was satisfied with the letter. It is still uncertain whether he ever got the letter sent to him in the care of Davydov, the book-seller. And so the quarrel ended, but unfortunately the two enemies remained unreconciled until——

(*Recorded from Lev Nikolaevich's words, January 23, 1877.*)

THE RECONCILIATION BETWEEN L. N. TOLSTOY AND I. S. TURGENEV

Written August 12, 1878.

With the religious influence growing within him, it made him particularly unhappy to think that there could still be a man who considered him as an enemy.

In the spring he sent a letter to Turgenev in Paris asking him to forget all the unfriendliness that had passed between them, and to remember only their former relations during the early stage of L. N.'s literary career when he had loved Turgenev sincerely. He even wrote in his letter : " If I am to blame in any way, forgive me." Turgenev answered very warmly : " I gladly shake the hand you offer me " —and promised to see us during his next visit to Russia.

On August 6 we returned from Samara, and received a wire from Turgenev announcing his arrival on the eighth. L. N. went to Tula to meet him, but I know nothing of their meeting there. Turgenev is a gentle, white-haired old man, who charmed us with the eloquence and picturesqueness with which he described both the simplest and the most sublime subjects. He described Antokolsky's statue of Christ so vividly that we actually seemed to see it before us ; later on he told us about his dog, Pegasus, with the same mastery of description. Turgenev's weakness of character has now become very obvious, but it is a weakness which is naïve and almost childlike. At the same time, he is very kind and gentle. This weakness of character really explains the whole quarrel with L. N.

For instance, he admits quite candidly that he is terribly afraid of cholera. At dinner there were thirteen at table, and we joked as to who would die first and who was afraid of death. Turgenev put up his hand and said, with a laugh :

" Que celui qui craint la mort lève la main."

No one put up his hand, except L. N., and he, too, did it out of politeness, saying :

" Eh bien, moi aussi je ne veux pas mourir."

Turgenev stayed two days. They did not mention the past, but talked and argued on abstract subjects. L. N. was very friendly and courteous to him, but seemed to avoid any real intimacy. As Turgenev was leaving, he said to me : " *Au revoir*. I am very happy to have been with you."

He kept his promise ; it was *au revoir*, for he came again at the beginning of September.

THE DIARY
1862-91

THE DIARY*

1862-91

October 8, 1862.

A diary once again. It makes me sad to go back to the old habits which I gave up when I got married. I used to take to writing whenever I felt depressed, and I am probably doing it now for the same reason. I have been feeling frightened ever since yesterday when he told me he did not believe in my love. I know why he doesn't believe in it, only I don't think I'll be able to put it into words. Ever since my early girlhood I have dreamed of a man *as a whole*, a new and *pure* man whom I would love. Those were childish dreams, but I still find it hard to give up the idea of loving a man who would always be with me, whose slightest thought and feeling I would know, who would love no one but me, and who, like myself, and unlike all other people, would not need *to sow his wild oats* before becoming good and sound. These dreams were always dear to me. As a result, I almost fell in love with P.; in other words, loving my dreams, I connected P. with them.

It wouldn't have been hard to go still further and to feel it even more intensely; but then I never really stopped, but went on without thinking. When I got

* The translator has made no attempt to "improve" the hurried style of the *Diary*, and, if some passages in it appear to be disjointed and incoherent, it is because they are so in the original. The illogical sequence of some of the sentences betrays, indeed, some of the most interesting temperamental peculiarities of the writer of the *Diary*.—A. W.

married, I had to admit that my old dreams were foolish, and yet I feel unable to give them up altogether. The *whole* of my husband's past is so dreadful that I don't think I will ever be able to accept it. Unless, of course, I acquire some new interest in life, such as children, whom I want terribly, for they alone will give me a *sound* future and will enable me to see things in a pure light, without his past, without all the filth which I still see in him, and which makes me so unhappy.

He doesn't understand that his past is a whole world of a thousand different emotions—good and bad—which will never belong to me, just as his youth, spent heaven knows on what and whom, will never be my property. Nor does he understand that I am giving him everything, that no part of my self has been spent elsewhere, and that only my childhood alone did not belong to him. But even that did. My fondest childhood reminiscence is my first love for him. Am I to blame that it was so cruelly destroyed? Was it wrong of me? He had spent his life and his energy on so much evil before he began to feel real love; and now he thinks it so strong and so pure, because for many, many years past he has been unable to feel it. There is some evil in my past, too, but not so much.

He likes to torture me and to see me weep because he has no faith in me. He would like me to have gone through as much evil as himself, so that I might more fully appreciate the good. It instinctively annoys him that I should have gained happiness so easily, without reflection, without previous suffering. I am going to be strong enough not to weep. I don't want him to see that I suffer; let him believe that I am always happy. Yesterday, at Grandfather's house, I came downstairs specially to see him, and when I saw him I was seized with an unusual feeling of love and strength. I loved him so much at that moment ; I wanted to go up to him, and yet I felt that if I touched him I would not feel so happy, that it would be almost sacrilege. But I never can and never will let him see what is going on in my mind. I have so much foolish pride that everything will be lost if I ever see that he can in the least doubt me. I am irritated. What is he doing to me ? Gradually I shall retreat into myself and shall poison his life. And yet I feel so sorry for him at those times when he doesn't believe in me ; his eyes fill with tears and he has such a meek, wistful look. At such moments I could strangle him with love, and yet the thought pursues me : "He doesn't believe in me, he doesn't believe in me." And to-day I suddenly felt that we would gradually drift apart and each live our own lives, that I would create my own sad world for myself, and he a world full of work and doubt. And this relationship struck me as vulgar. I have stopped believing in his love. When he kisses me, I think to myself : "Well, I'm not the first woman." And it begins to hurt me that this love of mine, my first and last, should not be enough for him. I, too, have been interested in men, but only in my imagination ; but he—he has known women, young and lively and pretty, with individual faces, souls, and characters, and he has loved and admired them, just as he now loves and admires me. It is vulgar ; but it isn't my fault ; it is the fault of his past. I cannot help it if I can't forgive God for having made people in such a fashion that they must sow their wild oats before becoming decent. I can't help it if it makes me feel sad and miserable that my husband, too, should come within that category. To make matters worse, he believes that I don't love him. But if I didn't love him, why should I be anxious to know what interested him in the past and what may interest him in the future ? It's a hopeless situation to try to prove one's love to a man who seems to think that he got married in spite of himself, and without being loved by his wife. As if there had ever been a moment in my life when I regretted any bit of the past or when I even dreamed of not loving him or of ceasing to love him ? Surely, it doesn't make him happy to see me weep and to make me realise that there is something wrong in our relations, and that, sooner or later, we will drift apart in the spiritual sense. What is a toy to the cat is tears to the mouse. But I am a frail toy, and, if you break it, it will be you who will weep. No, I can't stand the thought of this slow torture. He is so good and kind ! Everything evil repels him and he cannot tolerate it himself. In the past, I could admire all that was good and lovely, but now it is quite different ; no sooner do I grow joyful than he seems to damp my enthusiasm.

October 9.

We had a heart-to-heart talk yesterday, and I am feeling more at ease, even happier. We had such a fine ride to-day, and yet I still feel oppressed. I had some depressing dreams last night, and, though I don't remember them very clearly, my heart is heavy. I thought of Mother to-day, and I grew terribly sad, though, on the whole, I am happy. I don't regret the past, but always bless it. I have known much happiness in my life. My husband seems to have calmed down and to believe in me, may God grant it. I can see, of course, that I am not giving him very much happiness. If I woke up, I should become a different person. But I don't know how that can be done. He would then see how much I love him, I should know how to *tell* him of my love ; I should be able, as in the past, to look clearly into his soul and to realise how I could make him happy. I simply must wake up. This sleep came over me last summer when we drove from Pokrovskoye to Ivitsy. Then I woke up for a short time, but on our return to Moscow I again fell asleep, and haven't been awake since. Something seems to be hanging over me ; it seems to me that I shall soon die. This is strange, now that I have a husband. I listen to him sleeping, and I am frightened to be left alone. He won't let me go near him, which is sad ; physical things disgust him.

October 11.

I am terribly sad and take refuge in myself. My husband is ill, bad-tempered, and doesn't love me. I expected it, and yet I didn't know it would be so dreadful. I wonder where people get the idea of my immense happiness. No one seems to know that I am unable to create happiness either for him or for myself. When I am very sad, I sometimes say to myself : "What's the good of living when neither of us is happy." And now this thought keeps on recurring, and it frightens me. He grows colder and colder every day, while I go on loving him more and more. His coldness will soon become unbearable. He is too candid to deceive me. If he doesn't love me, we won't pretend, and when he does love me, I can see it in his every movement. To-day, Grisha " began to talk of *his papa*, and I felt so sorry that he wasn't a *real* son that I nearly wept. I often think of my people and how happy I was then, and now my heart breaks at the thought that no one loves me. Petya loves me merely as a matter of duty, and my husband has stopped loving me at all. My dear mother and Tanya, how sweet they were ! Why did I leave them ? It hurts me terribly to think of all the torture through which poor Lisa has had to go. Lyova* is wonderful, and I really feel that it is *all* my fault, and I am afraid to show him how sad I am ; such silly melancholy always annoys husbands. I sometimes try to console myself with the thought that it will pass and that everything will yet be right, but now I feel that it will not pass and that things will only go from bad to worse. Father writes to me : " Your husband loves you passionately." Yes, he did love me *passionately*, but passion dies, and no one except myself can understand that he was attracted to me without loving me. Why didn't I realise then that he would have to pay too heavy a price for it, for is it not terrible to live one's whole life with a wife one does not love ? Why did I ruin him, whom everybody loves ? It was selfishness on my part to have married him. Now that I look at him, I think the same that he used to think about me : I want to love him and yet I can't.

All this time has gone past like a dream. They tempted me by saying : " See how happy you can

* Henceforth Tolstoy will almost invariably be referred to as Lyova or Lyovochka, diminutives of Lev.

be." All that I once possessed has gone : my energy to work, my joy in life, my household talents. Now I only want to sit here all day long doing nothing and thinking of all kinds of sad things. I wanted to work, and I couldn't ; what's the good of putting on a silly bonnet which merely gives me a headache ? I want to play the piano, but it's awkward upstairs, for it'll be heard all over the house, and the piano down here is too bad. He suggested to-day that I stay at home while he went to Nikolskoye.[35] I should have agreed, and so rid him of my presence, and yet I wasn't strong enough to do it. I can hear him now, upstairs, playing a duet with Olga. Poor Lyova ! Always looking for amusements so as to be away from me. What good am I in this world ?

November 13.

An unlucky date ! Such was my first thought. I always feel easier after a heart-to-heart talk. Being an egoist, it gives me some satisfaction to torture him.

I can't find any occupation for myself. He is lucky to be so clever and talented. But I'm neither the one nor the other. One can't live on love alone ; and I am so stupid that I can do nothing but think of him. He is unwell, and I begin to believe that he will die, and that is enough to make me miserable for three hours. When he is cheerful, it makes me so glad, and I am only afraid lest his happy mood pass. When he is away or working, I always think of him, listening for his footsteps ; and when he is here, I keep watching his face. It is probably due to my pregnancy that I am in this abnormal state, which, to a certain extent, affects him too. It isn't hard to find work, but before doing anything one has to create some enthusiasm for breeding hens, tinkling the piano, and reading a lot of silly books and a very few good ones, or pickling cucumbers and what not. All this will come in time, when I forget my lazy old life and get used to the country. I don't want to get into the common rut and be bored ; but I shan't be. I wish my husband had a greater influence over me. It's strange that I should love him so much and yet feel his influence so little. There are some lucid moments when I realise everything and realise what a fine world this is to live in, and how many pleasant duties depend upon me ; but the mood passes and I forget everything. I am waiting for the happy day when everything begins running smoothly like an engine, so that I can begin an active existence. It's strange that I should be looking forward to it as one looks forward to a holiday, or to the coming of summer. I am in such a state of inertia now that neither our trip to Moscow nor the thought of our future child has the slightest effect on me, nor does it bring me joy. I should like to know what can waken me or refresh me.

I haven't prayed for a long time. In the old days, I enjoyed even the external side of religion. I would often, on the quiet, light the wax candle in front of the ikon, adorn it with flowers, lock the door, and kneel before it for an hour or more. Now it all seems stupid and ludicrous, and yet I find pleasure in remembering it.

Latterly, everything has become so earnest and serious, but the impressions of my early life are still so vivid that it is difficult to forget them, and yet there is no way back to them. In a few years I shall have created a *woman's* world for myself, which I shall love even more, for it will contain my husband and my children, whom one loves even more than one's parents and brothers. But I haven't reached that stage yet. I am still wavering between the past and the future. My husband loves me too much to put me on a sound footing just yet ; it is difficult, anyway, and I will have to work it all out for myself ; besides, he feels that I have already changed. With a little effort I can again become what I was before, although no longer a maiden, but a woman, and when this happens, both he and I will be satisfied.

I am sure that Moscow will refresh me, and amidst my old life I shall clearly realise all the good of my present position—for the evil is all my own fault. But if only he would be patient during this painful period of transition. . . . I am alone now, and, as I look around, it saddens me. It is terrible to be alone. I am not used to it. My old home was always so full of life, but here, when he is out, everything seems dead. He is accustomed to solitude and can't understand this. He doesn't mind being alone, for he finds consolation not in the people around him, but in his work. However, I also shall get used to it in time. But I never hear any joyful voices around me ; it is as though everybody were dead. To make matters worse, he grows angry when I tell him that I don't like being left alone. This is unfair, but then he has never had a family and can never understand it. But I shall do my best to make him happy ; he is such a fine man and I am so much worse than he, and I love him and have nothing, nothing left in the world except him.

I am bored because I have no imagination, no

ressources of any kind, because I am used to a noisy, boisterous life, while I find nothing here except a deadly silence. But I'll get used to it ; one can get used to anything. In time I shall have a house full of joy and mirth, and shall have an earnest, busy existence, and rejoice in the happy youth of my children.

November 23.

He disgusts me with his People. I feel he ought to choose between me, i.e. the representative of the family, and his beloved People. This is egoism, I know. But let it be. I have given my life to him, I live *through* him, and I expect him to do the same. Otherwise the place grows too depressing ; I ran away to-day because everybody and everything repelled me—Auntie and the students [36] and N. P.[37] and the walls and the whole life here, so that I laughed for joy when I ran quietly away from the house. L. did not disgust me, but I suddenly felt that he and I were miles apart, i.e. that his People could never absorb *all* my attention, while I couldn't take up all his attention, as he does mine. It's quite clear. If I am no good to him, if I am merely a doll, a *wife*, and not a *human being*—then it is all useless and I don't want to carry on this existence. Of course I am idle, but I am not idle by nature ; I simply haven't yet discovered what I can do here. He is angry and impatient. Oh, but never mind ! I am feeling free and happy to-day, and, although he was very gloomy, he didn't touch me. I know he is brilliant, poetic, and intelligent, full of *power*, but it annoys me that he should look at everything from a gloomy angle. I sometimes want to break loose from his somewhat sombre influence, to ignore it—but I can't. His influence is depressing because I begin to think in his way, to see things with his eyes, and I am afraid of losing my own self and yet not becoming like him. In future I shall go out or drive somewhere whenever I feel bored. Sometimes, when I go out, I suddenly feel so free. At other times I begin to imagine him worried and searching for me, and this depresses me so much that I come back home.

He was so gloomy that I nearly wept. He won't speak to me. It is terrible to live with him. What if he once again suddenly develops an affection for his People, and begins to love me no more than his school, nature, the People, or his literature—a little of everything, until the time comes when he'll start again looking for something new. Auntie came in to ask me why I had gone out and where I had been ; I wanted to annoy her, and told her I had run away from the students, whom she always shields and protects. It isn't true ; I don't mind the students at all, and I grumble and get annoyed because it's an old habit of mine. I went out simply because I was bored sitting indoors for so long ; I have never been used to it. There's no end to N. P. and Auntie and N. P. again, and the students. My husband is dumb and isn't mine to-day at all. Therefore, he *isn't there*. I wish I could go away, see how they are all keeping at home, and then come back again. I'll go and play the piano again. He is in his bath just now ; he's a stranger to me to-day.

December 6, 1862.

Some day I shall kill myself with jealousy. " Never so much in love as now ! " [28] And nothing but a big fat lump of a woman. Terrible ! I kept looking at his daggers and rifles with the greatest joy. One jerk —it's so easy. So long as there is no child. And there she is, a few yards from here. It drives me mad ! I shall go out for a drive. I may meet her at any moment. So that's how he loved her ! If only I could burn his diary and his whole past !

I have come back, and am feeling worse than ever. I've got a headache and my heart is heavy. I felt so happy and free in the wide open air. I want to be able to live and breathe freely, and think freely. But life is so petty. But love is difficult, and the love that takes one's breath away, a love that is complete, that lasts for ever—that is impossible. If it weren't for him, this little world of mine would be narrow and miserable. And yet it is impossible to unite our two little worlds into one. He is so clever, so active, so brilliant —and then there is that terrible long past of his. I am terrified at the thought of going to Moscow now. I will become even more insignificant, and I feel that, if there is ever to be a world which will satisfy me, it must be here, in Yasnaya Polyana, with no people from outside, but merely my own family and all that I will create for myself.

I have read the beginnings of some of his books, and each time he speaks of love and women I begin to feel disgusted and depressed and want to burn all, all that he has written. May I never be reminded of his past ! And I wouldn't care about his books, for jealousy makes me a fearful egoist.

If I could kill him and then make another man exactly like him, I should do it joyfully.

January 9, 1863.

Never before has the consciousness of my guilt made me feel so unhappy. I never thought I could be so guilty. I am so depressed that the tears have been choking me all day. I am afraid to look at him or to speak to him. Never has he been so dear and precious to me, and never have I felt so mean and loathsome. He is not angry, he still loves me, and he has such a gentle and sacred expression in his eyes. I could die of happiness and humility in the presence of such a man. I am feeling very ill. The mental pain has brought on physical pain. I felt so ill that I thought I would have a miscarriage. I have become almost insane. I keep praying all day long as if this would lessen my guilt and bring back what is gone. I feel easier when he isn't here. I can weep then and love him, but when he is here I am tortured by the pangs of conscience, and it is agony to watch his face and his kind look, which I love so much, but which I have been avoiding ever since last night. How can I ever cause him such annoyance? I kept wondering how I could cover up my guilt—cover up is a silly word—I mean, how I could become more fit for him. I cannot love him any more than I do, because I love him to the uttermost limit, with all my soul, and I have no other thought in my mind, no other desire—nothing at all, beyond my love for him. There is no evil in him of which I might accuse him. He doesn't believe that I can do without amusements—but I need nothing,

nothing at all except him. If only he knew how happy it makes me to think of the future, not with " amusements," but with him, and all that is dear to him. I even try to like everything and everybody I didn't like before—Auerbach, for instance. I was in a particularly bad temper yesterday ; I quite surpassed myself. Surely I haven't such a vicious temper? Isn't it all the effect of my nerves and of this pregnancy ? But it doesn't matter, for at least I know that I am *guarding our happiness*, unless I have already ruined it. This is terrible. Everything might have been so joyful and happy. He is well now ; but what have I done !

Tanya, Sasha, and K.[39] have arrived. I still can't keep myself from weeping. I shan't let them see me ; they are children and have never been in love. How anxiously I am waiting for him ! But what if he grows cold to me ? Oh, God ! Now everything, absolutely everything, depends on him. I am so mean and unworthy, and this mental pettiness weighs heavily on me. It must suddenly have struck him how miserable and insignificant I am.

January 11, 1863.

I feel a little more at ease, for his treatment of me has much improved. But the sorrow is still fresh in my mind, and everything reminding me of it brings on intense physical pain. It is physical, because I can feel it run down all my nerves and veins. He didn't say anything, and did not even allude to my diary. I don't know if he has read it. I feel that it is horrible, and even I find it unpleasant to re-read.

I am quite alone and I am frightened, and meant

to write sincerely and at great length, but fright has scattered my thoughts. In view of my pregnancy I am afraid of any shocks. My jealousy is an innate disease, or it may be due to the fact that, loving him, I love nothing else and have given myself to him so completely that I can be happy only with him. I fear to lose him, as old people fear to lose the only child on whom their whole life depends, and whom they can't have again if they lose him. I had always been told that I was not an egoist, yet isn't this the highest form of egoism ? I am not an egoist in anything else, but in this respect I am a terrible one.

But I love him so much that that, too, will pass. Only it will require an immense amount of patience and will-power ; otherwise it will be no good. There are days when I love him almost morbidly. This is one of these days. It is always when I feel guilty. It hurts me to look at him, to listen to him ; I feel like a devil in the presence of saints. When I can do anything to please him and to make him love me as before, our relations will again become more simple and straightforward. But now our merits are unequal, and therefore there must also be this difference in our relationship. Merits, of course, are never quite equal, but if only there were a little less evil on my side ! I used to love him boldly, with self-assertion, but now I thank him, and God, for every kind word he utters, every caress, every lenient, gentle look.

Now I just live for all this, waiting for his kindness, and it is all I need. I used to be full of pride at the thought of the child inside me, but that is merely fate and a law of nature. There's no consolation in this, either. All I have is my husband, Lyova, who is everything to me, who is responsible for that merit of mine; I love him terribly, and nothing matters except him.

Moscow, January 14, 1863.

I'm alone again and feeling sad. But all has been happily settled between us. I don't know what exactly reconciled him to me, or what reconciled me to him, But it just came about naturally. All I know is that my happiness has been restored. I should like to go home. I often build up plans of my future life in Yasnaya *with him*. But it makes me feel very sad to think how much I have broken away from the Kremlin folks. I am terribly conscious of the fact that my whole world has changed, and yet I love them more than ever, especially Mother, and I sometimes feel sorry that I have ceased to be a member of their family. I live for him, and it sometimes saddens me to think that I am not *everything* to him, and that, if I suddenly died, he would soon find consolation; for he is full of *ressources*, while I am but an insignificant creature: once I have adopted a world as my own, I should never be able to find another.

I find the hotel life depressing. I never feel happy except when I'm with my family *and with Lyova*. I could soon go back home, for it largely depends on me; and yet I haven't the courage to say good-bye so soon, and I'm also too lazy to move.

I had such an unpleasant dream last night. I dreamed of an immense garden into which all our Yasnaya village girls came, and all of them were dressed up like ladies. They all went off somewhere, one by one, and the last one to leave was A., wearing a black silk dress. I talked to her, but grew so angry that, taking her child from somewhere, I began to tear it to pieces. In a terrible rage I tore off its arms and its head. Lyova came in and said that they would exile me to Siberia, and then picked up the hands and legs and all the parts, and said that, after all, it didn't matter, for it was only a doll. I looked, and, indeed, it was all cloth and cotton-wool. This annoyed me greatly.

It tortures me to think of her, even here in Moscow. I am not tortured by jealousy—but it's all that *past.* He will never be mine as completely as I am his, for his past is great, rich, and varied, and, even if he died now, his life would still have been a full one. Paternity is the only thing he has never experienced. Now life has suddenly given me so much of what I had never known before, that I cling on to my happiness for fear of losing it. I have never known such happiness before, and have no faith that it will last. It always seems to me that it is momentary and accidental—for it is too wonderful. It is very strange that one man, with nothing but his personality, and quite apart from any other qualities, should have been able to take me in hand and make me so intensely happy.

Mother is quite right—I have become sillier than ever, or, rather, my brain has become too lazy. It is most unpleasant to feel so apathetic. The physical life does indeed affect the mental.

I regret the loss of my old vivaciousness. But I believe that it will come back. I feel sure that it would have as good an effect on Lyova as it once had on my own family. During the first few weeks at Yasnaya

I was still very lively, but now it has gone. Lyova loved me so much in my playful moods. Lyova, too, seems to be mentally asleep, though I know quite well that his mind never really rests. He has grown very thin, and this worries me. I would give a lot to be able to see inside his mind. He has even stopped writing his diary, which is a great pity.

I sometimes have a silly, unconscious desire to test my power over him ; it is simply a desire to see him obey me. But he will always be stronger than me, and my desire for self-assertion will pass.

Moscow, January 17, 1863.

I have just been in a bad mood, and have been angry that he should love everybody and everything, while I want him to love only me. Now I have come home, and realised that it was only my silly whim ; he is such a good man, with a great wealth of emotion. Now that I come to think of it, the real source of all my troubles and bad moods is my egoism and my idea that his whole life, his thoughts, and his love must belong to me. It's the rule with me : no sooner do I begin to get fond of something than I pull myself up by reminding myself that I love nothing and no one except Lyova. And yet one ought to have something else to love as well, just as Lyova loves his *work*, so that I could turn to it whenever he is cold to me. Such moments are bound to come more and more frequently ; but in reality it has been like this all the time. I can see it quite clearly now, for I have nothing else to occupy my mind ; he, of course, is too busy to notice all the details of our relationship. But at least this helps me to learn how to behave with him—not consciously, but spontaneously, and, although I am still unable to apply this knowledge in practice, that will come in time. I want to go back to Yasnaya, where more of his life is devoted to me. There is no one else there except me and Auntie. I love the life there, and wouldn't exchange it for anything. My only wish is to devote myself to it. I shall gradually arrange things so that I shall be utterly happy, and I know I can keep Lyova quite happy there, as long as he doesn't want outside people, for I won't be able to get them for him, and, in any case, I don't like them. But, if Lyova really wants it, I can keep an open house and receive anybody he wants. The main thing is to make him happy and contented, for then he loves me, and that is all I want. It is difficult to live together without quarrelling, but, all the same, I shan't quarrel, for L. is quite right in saying that a quarrel between husband and wife makes a *cut* which never heals. My greatest misfortune is my jealousy. We must both watch this very carefully. He doesn't always want to take me with him ; a hat and crinoline, all this gets on his nerves, and yet I always feel so lonely when he is away. I'm afraid of clinging to him ; if only he would always feel the need for my company, since my longing to see him grows stronger every day.

I have waited and waited for him, and now I have sat down again to write. There must be people who can live in solitude, but it is terrible to be alone. I don't suppose we'll go to the lecture now. Perhaps I was in his way ? This thought is always troubling me, for in most cases it is my own fault. I have developed an extraordinary love for my mother, and the thought of it terrifies me, for we shall never again be able to live together. Nowadays my love for Tanya has a tinge of superiority about it, as if it was my right. It is terrible to have to leave them again. Lyova doesn't understand this, and I don't talk about it to him. I like Auntie very well these days, especially as I haven't been discussing her with Lyova ; he is far too partial. I feel sorry that I have not been nicer to her, for, after all, she nursed Lyova, and is going to nurse my own children. It's a wise thing to be nice to people, for they love you for it. The trouble is that I am always afraid to flatter people when I don't quite mean it. But, after all, there is nothing insincere in being nice and respectful to a good, kindly old woman like Auntie. I have become very one-sided. Nothing interests me beyond our own life—and, of course, the people and the surroundings with which we come in touch. It is past 2 o'clock, and he still hasn't arrived. Why, then, make promises ? Isn't it wrong that he should be so unpunctual ? It must be all right, for it shows that he isn't petty. I don't like to see him in a temper. He just pierces you with his words—it is better to keep out of his way at such moments. But his temper never lasts, and he very seldom grumbles.

Moscow, January 29, 1863.

I find this life in the Kremlin depressing, for it reminds me of my lazy and aimless life before my marriage. I have no longer any illusions about the aims and duties of married life since Lyova let me see that it alone isn't sufficient, but that one needs other interests as well. [A note added in Tolstoy's own handwriting : *I don't want anything except you. Lyova talks a lot of nonsense !*]

March 3, 1863.

The same old story : I am alone and busy writing. But I am not lonely ; I have become used to it. I have the happy conviction that he loves me, and loves me constantly. When he comes back, he always comes up to me so kindly, asking me some question or telling me something. Life has become happy and cheerful for me. I read his diary, and it made me happy. Two things—I and his work ; he cares for nothing else. He has been in such an occupied mood yesterday and to-day. I'm afraid to disturb him when he is busy writing and thinking. I'm afraid that if he gets annoyed he will become dissatisfied with my presence. I'm glad he is writing. I wanted to drive to Mass to-day, but in the end I stayed at home and prayed here. Since I am married I find ritual and everything false even more objectionable than before. I long with all my heart to work about the house and be of *use*. Only I don't know how to begin. But it will all come in time. And yet I have been fussing around, pretending to myself and everybody else that I am very busy. I shouldn't have done that. Besides, what's the good of deceiving people ? Sometimes I know perfectly well what I *ought* to do and how I can spend my time profitably, but then I think of other things and forget about it. Life has become so easy and simple ! I feel all the time that my whole life and *duties* are bound up with Yasnaya, and I want nothing more. And if I were asked, even at a moment of depression, what I wanted, I shouldn't know what to say. I don't think

I have a real affection for Auntie, and this makes me sad. Her old age irritates me more often than it makes me feel sorry for her. That is bad. She often loses her temper and is insincere. It is so sunny outside—as sunny as in my heart. I am gradually becoming used to everything—to the students, to the common people, to Auntie, and even to all the things that used to annoy me before. Lyova's influence is strong, and it gives me joy to realise it.

March 26, 1863.

I am unwell, and in a state of apathy. He went to Tula in the morning, and it seems as though I haven't seen him for a month. I don't seem to have been happy for a very, very long time. And I feel as though he weren't here at all, merely his shadow or his phantom. Deep down in my soul I love him, and I feel this love as strongly as ever, and I know that it is still the one thing in my life. I went round the servants' quarters ; it depressed me terribly. They are all ill, and miserable, and full of complaints. But there are also some sly foxes among them, which made me even sadder. Auntie is in a peaceful, friendly state of mind, and yet I find her wearisome—she is so old. I have been thinking about my own people. They have such a full life. I sometimes miss them, but I never regret the past. I am so happy now. I am often afraid to love him, for it is so easy to spoil a happiness like mine. It fills me with anxiety to realise that he hasn't returned yet. Each time I don't go out with him I start reproaching myself for having stayed at home. I begin to think that it would be better to annoy him and to be in his way than to stay at home, worrying.

It's the same every time. He mustn't go to Nikolskoye, or it'll drive me insane. If only people would realise how slowly the time passes. Auntie has just been here and kissed my hand. Why did she do it ? I was deeply touched. She is a kind soul, and must feel sorry for me because I am left all alone. When she's in a temper she gets bilious attacks. I am young and should tolerate her little weaknesses, and my conscience sometimes troubles me for being impatient and irritable with her.

He was annoyed yesterday, but didn't say anything. This must mean that there is something unnatural in our relations. Now, I always like to tell him when anything worries or irritates me, but I am sometimes afraid. I am spoilt. Lyova gives me too much happiness. I love everything about him : his cheerful moods, as well as his bad moods, his kind, kind face, his meekness, and his impatience—everything ! His face expresses everything so beautifully, that he *hardly* ever hurts my feelings. I am so comfortable here, writing down these notes almost mechanically, and thinking of him and remembering him in so many different attitudes, with so many different expressions. This scribbling is merely a means of concentration ; it helps me to imagine him more vividly. Whenever he returns I feel almost morbidly joyful. But, whatever he may say, he can never love me as much as I love him. He wouldn't wait for me with the same feeling of patient worry.

April 1.

I am unwell and bored. Lyova has gone off. It is a great misfortune to have no *ressources* within one's self. It's a very important thing to possess. It is beautiful summer weather outside, and my mood is like the summer—sad. Everything around me seems empty and lonely. Lyova has his work and his farming to think about, but there is nothing to keep my mind busy. What am I capable of, anyway? I can't go on living like this. I should like some more work to do. Some *real* work. In weather like this I always used to long for something, and dream about heaven knows what. But now I don't want anything; I have no more of that silly longing to go somewhere, for I instinctively feel that I have found everything and that there is nothing else to seek, and yet I sometimes feel a little bored. Much happiness and little work. And one grows tired even of the good things. One needs some work, if only as a matter of contrast. What was reverie and fancy ought now to become serious work—a *real* life, not merely a life of the imagination. Everything is so silly; it annoys me.

April 8, 1863.

Lyova and I have started working on the estate; he's taking it seriously, I—more or less pretending to. It is all very fine and joyful, and *not petty*. I am greatly interested in everything, and much of it gives me joy. But he seems to be worried, depressed, and unwell, and this makes me continuously anxious. But I'm afraid to tell him how worried I am about his blood pressure. It is terrible to think of it, and yet I can't help imagining that all this life of ours, all this immense happiness, may merely be a trick of Fate who may all of a sudden snatch it all away. I am afraid of it. . . . It's silly, but I can't write this down. I wish this fear would disappear quickly. It poisons my whole existence. He has bought some bees, which makes me glad ; all this management of the estate is very interesting, though difficult.

The Auerbachs and —— are very boring ; I could do so well without any visitors at all. She bored me terribly, but for some reason I feel sorry for her. I wonder if she loves her husband ? But with some people marriage is a real *mystery*. There's something the matter with Lyova. He seems to have become insincere and unnatural. Or is it merely his headaches ? What's the matter with him ? What does he want ? I'd do anything he wanted, if only I could. He is away now, but I'm already frightened in case he comes back in a bad temper and something annoys him. I love him terribly, I know it, for I could tolerate anything from him, if ever there were anything to tolerate.

April 10, 1863.

He has gone to Tula to meet Father, and I am already feeling lonely. I have been reading over his letters to V. A.[40] He was young then, and didn't love her, for he was still fond of his loving family circle in those days. I recognise him so well in everything : in his moral canons and his constant striving towards the good. What a charming man ! After reading his letters, I somehow stopped being jealous, as though it weren't V. at all, but *myself*. I began to picture the whole thing to myself. She seems to have been a pretty girl, rather silly, and youthfully attractive (in the moral sense, of course), while he was just the same as now, not really loving V., but loving love and goodness. Sudakovo, too, has become clear to me, with its piano and sonatas, and the pretty little dark-haired girl, trusting and kind. And all that youth (why, what's that? I'm talking like an old woman!) and nature, and the solitude of the country. . . . It is all quite plain, and it doesn't make me feel sad. Then I read some of his plans for a family life. Poor Lyova, he was so young in those days, and did not know that happiness could not be *planned* in advance, and that it was bound to lead to disappointment. But what fine, noble thoughts!

April 28, 1863.

Lyova is either old or unhappy. I wonder if really nothing has any interest for him, beyond money, his estate, and his distillery?[41] Except when he eats or sleeps or sits in silence, he spends his time roaming about the estate, all alone. I am bored at always being left alone. He expresses his love for me by automatically kissing my hand, and by doing me good instead of evil.

The weather is fine, and I should be feeling cheerful, and yet I am depressed. In the old days, Tanya and I knew how to appreciate the spring and the summer, and we both enjoyed ourselves, and the more we could be together and share our thoughts the better we liked it. We didn't worry, then, how much the factory would cost, and what particular installations it would require; it is terribly boring. I shall be terribly glad when she comes. I love young people, especially such charming young people as Tanya. Lyova makes me feel embarrassed. I seem to feel shy and ashamed about everything. What can the reason be? My conscience is clear, and I have done nothing wrong. Even when I am writing down these thoughts, I feel embarrassed lest he may read them. I am afraid to love him, and afraid that he will see this, that I irritate him, and that all this doesn't matter to him. If I were asked what I wanted, I shouldn't be able to say. All these moods come to me of their own accord.

April 25.

All this morning I felt sad, and had a feeling that something terrible was going to happen. I am still as shy about Lyova. I had a terrible crying fit, though I didn't realise afterwards what had caused it; and yet at the time I knew there was good cause to weep, and even to die, if Lyova stopped loving me as he once did. I didn't want to write anything, and yet, as I was sitting downstairs, the old desire to scribble came over me. I have been interrupted. . . .

Evening of April 29.

I get annoyed about trifles. For instance, about the dresses that have been sent me. I make a great effort not to lose my temper, and I shall succeed before long. I feel terribly affectionate and a little shy towards Lyova; it is the result of my petty moods. I feel disgusted with myself. I haven't felt like this for a long time. I should love to look after the bees and the apple-trees, and to work on the estate and keep myself busy—and yet there is this constant feeling of boredom and weariness, and the helpless knowledge that I must stay quietly at home and take care of my body. It's annoying. It saddens me to think that this helplessness of mine makes Lyova feel so unfriendly towards me, as if it were my fault that I am pregnant. I can't be of assistance to him in anything. There is another thing that makes me feel disgusted with myself. (A diary must, above all, be truthful.) I enjoyed the idea of how V. V. was in love with me. I wonder if I should like anybody to fall in love with me now. How petty and disgusting ! I always made fun of him, and never felt any other way towards him—he disgusted me and I never respected him. Lyova is breaking away from me more and more. The physical side of love matters a great deal to him. That's dreadful—for it's exactly the other way round with me. But his morality is *sound*, and that is the main thing.

May 8, 1863.

My pregnancy is the cause of it all. I am in a terrible state both physically and mentally. I am always ill, and I feel mentally bored and depressed. I simply don't exist, so far as Lyova is concerned. I feel I am distasteful to him, and my only aim now is to leave him alone and to cut him out of my life as far as possible. I can bring him no joy of any kind so long as I am pregnant. How sad to discover that a wife can only learn during her pregnancy whether or not her husband really loves her. He is down among the beehives. I would give anything to be with him, and yet I'm not going, for I have terrible palpitations, and it is uncomfortable to sit there, and a thunderstorm is coming on, and I have a headache, and I'm bored—I want to weep and I don't want to annoy or bore him, especially now that he is ill himself. He makes me feel embarrassed most of the time. If he is kind to me at times, it is largely a matter of habit, which he still keeps up, though he has stopped loving me in the old way. He would find it hard to confess that he once loved me, and quite recently, too, but that it is all over now. But if only he knew how much he has changed ; if he could step into my shoes, he would soon realise what kind of life I am leading. But there is no help for it. He will wake up again after the baby is born. It's always like that. It's that terrible *common rut* of which we once were so much afraid. Unfortunately, I still love him terribly much, much more than ever. When will I ever get into that cursed rut too ?

May 9.

He promised to be here at 12, and now it is 2 o'clock. I wonder if anything has happened ? Why does he like to torture me like this ? It's a pity to chase even a friendly dog away. My mother's fate was rather like mine during the first year of her marriage. It was even worse for her, for while Lyova is merely busy on the estate, Father used to drive out, visiting patients and gambling. But, like her, I am ill and pregnant, and feel lonely and abandoned. Experience alone teaches. One's youth is more of a misfortune than a blessing—at any rate, when one is married. After all, you can't spend all day *in perfect solitude*, sewing and playing the piano, and gradually coming to the conclusion that you've got to stick where you are, even though your husband cares nothing for you. Mother said that she found life much more cheerful as she grew older ; and it was only when the children arrived that she found something to take up her mind. That's how it'll be with me, too. I know I'm ill-tempered and discontented—but it's merely because I've been waiting so anxiously for him ever since 12 o'clock. It's wicked of him to be so pitiless; anyone with even a slight feeling of pity in his heart would feel sorry for a person who suffers.

May 12.

I am making a great effort not to be bored, and, though I am not happy, I am calm and not too sad.

May 22.

When I come into this study without thinking, I am overcome by a feeling of cold and boredom. But when I walk in expecting it to be full of life, as it once was, it feels quite different. Now I feel cold and bored—or, rather, afraid. It's the fear of death and the fear that all our past is dead. There is no life when there is no love. As I ran about the garden yesterday, I wondered if I would have a miscarriage. No, I have an iron constitution. He feels no love for me whatsoever. He is ill now, but when he gets better, he, too, will begin to feel terrified. How rich one's imagination always is, and how poor one's life. One can *imagine* so many things—a thousand different worlds, and yet one has to live in one's own narrow little circle. I love mine and need nothing else, but he is tired of it, and has started longing for something different. I have come to the conclusion that I don't want anything except him. I have often thought it. Mother often used to say that there was nothing worse than keeping one's husband tied to one's apron-strings.

Those are true words. I ought to worship her ; she has suffered so much in her life. It is hard to live—one has to be made of steel. And one has to work out very carefully how to live. Before I was married I used to think that it was best to live without love. I knew well that I could not love *a little*, and that it was painful to love too much. Tanya knew that, too ; she doesn't gain happiness easily, either. She is young and cheerful, and can live, with all her heart : she has a rich nature. I wonder if anybody will ever crush her ? She will not easily accept a life that gives her too little. But she is more capable than I am of inspiring love. I always *cut* it myself, quite against my will, and I have to pay for it. Every *cut* takes away a bit of my life, i.e. a little of my strength, of my youth, of my energy and joy, and makes me despise myself more. And the cut can never be healed. I must treasure *his* love. It lingers on, but very feebly ; or perhaps it has ceased altogether. That is terrible, and I always keep thinking of it. I have been ill ever since yesterday. I am afraid of a miscarriage, and yet the pain in my belly gives me pleasure. It was the same in my childhood. Although Mother would forgive me for some misdeed, I wouldn't forgive myself and pinch my hand and prick it with a needle as a punishment. Though the pain becomes unbearable, I endure it with an intense feeling of pleasure. This is the right time for putting love to the test. When good weather and good health come back, life will become more orderly. I will take pride in the house, in the baby, and ——* will come back, too—that's disgusting.

And he will think that, although love has returned,

* Two words left out in the Russian edition.

his wife hasn't, and he will merely remember her. And then again he will be unwell and worried, and bored with that hateful wife of his, always there in front of his eyes. That's the kind of life which awaits him. As for my own life, it is all gone ; it is nothing but a remembrance of the love I had for him and of the thought that he may love me yet. I'm a fool to have believed it and to have prepared so much suffering for myself. Everything seems so miserable. The clock strikes mournfully, the dog is sad, Dushka is so unhappy, and the two old women are both so miserable, and everything is dead. And if Lyova——

June 6.

A lot of young people have arrived and have disturbed our life ; I am sorry. None of them seem to be very cheerful. Is it because everything is so *cold*? It all affects me quite differently from what I expected. They did not cheer me up ; they merely made me more nervous, and things have become even drearier. I love Lyova immensely, but it annoys me that I should have accepted this unequal rôle in our relationship. I am entirely dependent on him, and God knows how I treasure his love. But he either takes mine for granted or else doesn't need it, for he seems to be alone all the time. I feel as though *everything* were over and that autumn was coming. But I don't know what *everything* means. I don't know what kind of a winter there will be after autumn, or whether there will be any at all—I can't picture it. It's so annoying that I should have no desires, that nothing can give me joy, as though I had become an old woman—old age is unbearable. I no longer wanted to go out driving after he said to me, " You and I, the old ones, will stay at home." I was so happy to stay alone with him once again. As if I were in love with him, and were not allowed to be. Now they have driven away, and Lyova has gone out, and I am alone again, and bored and miserable. I feel annoyed, and am prepared to accuse him of being thoughtless and of not having bought a carriage for me, and so on, and to tell him that the best thing for him to do is to leave me lying on the sofa with a book, and to take no further notice of me. But, when I stop being annoyed, I realise that he has lots of work to do, that he really hasn't time to trouble about me, that the work on the estate is like convict labour, and, in addition to it all, there are all these visitors who don't give him a moment's peace. That repulsive fellow, Anatole,[43] keeps hanging around. It isn't his fault if they cheated him about the carriage—he is such a fine, *wonderful* man, and I love him with all my soul.

June 7.

I love him madly ; this emotion has taken such a powerful hold on me. He is always working about the house ; but I am not bored ; I'm feeling very happy. He loves me now—I think I can feel it. I wonder if this doesn't mean an early death for me. It will be sad and terrible to leave him. The more I get to know him, the better I love him. Every day I feel that I love him more than ever before. Nothing exists for me except him and his concerns.

June 8.

Lyova is terribly cheerful. Solitude kills him, while the company of people livens him up immensely. No, sir, I'm much stronger than you! His illness was merely the effect of boredom. Tanya is very unwell, and both Sashas are in very delicate health, especially mine.

July 17, 1863.

It's all over now; the child is born. My suffering is at an end, and I am gradually entering into life again, but with a constant feeling of dread and anxiety about the child, and especially about my husband. I am obsessed with a new painful feeling which will always torture me: it seems to be the fear of not doing my duty towards *my family*. I have become afraid of my husband, as though I were to blame for something. I feel that I am weighing heavily on him, that I am stupid (the same old song!), and even vulgar and commonplace. I have become unnatural, for I fear the animal love of the mother for her child, and I'm afraid of my almost unnatural love for my husband. I try to hide all this; but this feeling of shame is false and stupid. I sometimes console myself with the thought that it is, after all, a good thing to love one's husband and children. I'm afraid I shall never go beyond that; though I should like to become a little more educated, if only for the sake of my husband and my children. How strong the maternal feeling can be! It doesn't seem strange at all, but quite natural that I am a mother. It's Lyova's child—that's why I love it. I am worried by Lyova's present state of mind. He has such a wealth of thought and feeling, and yet it is all being wasted. I appreciate his wonderful qualities only too well, and, heaven knows, I wish he could be happy in every way.

July 23.

I have now been married for ten months. I lose courage terribly. I automatically look for support, as the child looks for the breast. I am all doubled up with pain. Lyova is hopeless. He can't run the estate for anything—it isn't in his line. He is too restless. He still isn't satisfied with what he's got ; I know what he wants, but he shan't have it. Everything is so cheerless. I am used to his caresses, like a dog—but he has grown cold. I believe that such moods do occur. But it seems to happen too often. *Patience*. . . .

July 24.

I went out on to the balcony, and was seized with a feeling of almost painful joy. Nature was so fine, it reminded me of God, and everything seemed so vast and free. . . . The family have departed, as well as Mother, my best of friends. I didn't weep much—I still have the same feeling of apathy. My husband has cheered up, thank God. I have prayed so much for him. He loves me ; may God grant us strong, unchanging happiness. My pain is increasing, and, like a snail, I have retired into my shell, determined to suffer to the end. I love the child very much ; it would poison my life if I had to stop nursing it. I have a great longing to rest, to enjoy the open fields, and I feel like a prisoner in gaol. I am waiting anxiously for my husband's return from Tula. I love him with all my heart, with a good, steady love, though with a slight feeling of inferiority. I'm going, now, to sacrifice myself to the child. . . .

July 31.

He goes on uttering platitudes, which is terrible. Why should he be angry? Whose fault is it? " Our relations are frightful—at such a miserable time, too. He has become so unpleasant that I try all day long to avoid him. When he says: " I'm going to sleep," or " I'm going for a bathe," I say to myself, " Thank God." When I look at the boy, my heart breaks. God has taken from me both my husband and my child; and yet we both prayed so fervently. . . . Everything seems to be at an end. But patience! At any rate, I can always bless our past. I have loved him deeply, and feel grateful to him for everything. I have just been reading his diary. . . . Everything seems wrong to him. *These past nine months are about the worst in my life*—to say nothing of the tenth one. How often has he said to himself: " Why did I get married," and how often has he said aloud, " What has become of my old self? "

August 2, 1863.

Not written for my feeble brains. . . . Wasting his time. . . . Wouldn't it be a good thing if you cleared out of here, Sophie Andreyevna? It makes me unhappy to be treated like this. I am determined never to mention him again. Perhaps it will pass off.

August 3.

I have talked to him, and I feel more at ease, for my assumption was right. It is revolting not to nurse one's own child—who says it isn't? But what can be done against a bodily defect? I instinctively feel that he is unjust to me. Why should he go on torturing me like this? I have become irritable; I don't even see my duty towards the baby in the same light to-day; and, just as he would like to wash me off the face of the earth because I am suffering and am not taking proper care of the child, so I don't want to see him because he goes on writing and doesn't suffer. Here's another aspect of the cruelty of husbands. I had never thought of this before. At this very moment I feel that I don't love him. One can't love a fly that keeps stinging one all the time. I can't improve matters, though I shall take care of the boy and shall do all within my power, though not for Lyova's sake, who ought to be paid out in his own coin. What a weakness on his part not to be able to be patient until I am better. I suffer and endure ten times as much as he. I wanted to write all this because I was in a temper.

It has started raining, and I'm afraid he will catch a cold. I am no longer angry; I love him—may God bless him.

[Added in Tolstoy's handwriting and then crossed out: *Sonya, forgive me, I now realise my fault, and I know how great it is. There are days when one seems to be guided not by one's own will, but by some irresistible outside power. That's why I treated you so badly—and to think it could have been me! I always knew that I had many faults, but thought that I at least had a tiny spark of feeling and generosity within me. And yet I could be cruel and unkind—and to whom? To the one being who has given me the greatest happiness in life and who alone loves me. Sonya, I know that one doesn't forgive and forget such things; but*

I know you better now, and realise more fully all my meanness. Sonya, my darling, I was unkind and revolting and . . . but there is a good man within me who sometimes falls asleep. Love him, Sonya, and don't blame him.]

Lyova wrote this, as he asked my forgiveness. But soon afterwards, he lost his temper and crossed it all out. It was at the time when I had those terrible pains in my breast and *was unable* to nurse Serezha. Surely, it wasn't that I *didn't want* to, when all I longed for was to be able to do it. I deserved those few lines of kindness and remorse, yet in his irritation against me he crossed them out before I had even time to read them.

August 17, 1863.

I have been meditating and remembering those *mad* nights of a year ago, when I was still so happy, joyful, and carefree. If ever I knew the full enjoyment of life, it was then. I loved, and I could feel and understand it all, and the whole world seemed so joyous and fresh. And, added to all this was the dear, poetic *comte*, with his deep, serene, and infinitely pleasant look (that was the impression he made then). What a wonderful time that was to me, thrilled by the vague suggestion of his love. . . . I must have felt it, or I couldn't have been so happy. One evening, I remember, when Popov was with us, he said something to me that hurt me terribly, and, wanting to show my independence, I went out into the garden and sat on the steps beside Popov, pretending to be very much interested in him, though I kept listening to the *comte's* conversation inside the house. Ever since then my affection for the *comte* began to grow, and I made it a rule never to be insincere towards him. I thought of all this to-day, and the knowledge that the *comte* was now my husband filled me with a strange feeling of happiness. Lisa knew well enough where happiness lay hidden, only Sonya Behrs didn't see it.[44] But now she knows it—with all her heart. He is so silly to be jealous.[45] Surely, good heavens, there was nothing that could have given him cause for it. I felt sorry that he had spent that poetic August of last year alone, and not with me. It might have been even more wonderful than it was. He is out now, and I always feel lonely when he is away. But I'll get used to it some day. I am waiting anxiously for my health to improve; it will be like a return to life—to my life with Lyova, for now we are separated. His doubts of my love for him always upset me terribly. How can I prove it when I love him so well, so steadfastly, so *honestly*.

September 10.

I am a little sad that my youth is gone, a little envious, and very bored. All the pain and the suffering of my life lies within these four walls; when I am outside I feel blissfully happy, and light-hearted, and so contented with my family life. Again the moon is shining and the nights are so warm and gentle, but they don't seem to belong to me. Nathalie's child is dying. The agony is terrible. Why all this suffering for the child and for the mother? And the father sobbing. I felt so sorry for them that I wept. Lyova's look pursues me wherever I go. At the piano yesterday, it made me shudder. What were his thoughts just then? I had never seen such an expression in his eyes before. Was he remembering anything about the past ?

Jealousy ? He loves——

September 22.

It'll be a year to-morrow since we were married. Then I looked forward to happiness, now I anticipate unhappiness. I had thought that all this about going to the war was a joke, but there seems to be something in it. It's most puzzling. He isn't eccentric, is he ? No ; but merely inconstant. I wonder whether it is consciously or unconsciously that he seems to be trying to arrange our life in such a way as to make me thoroughly unhappy ? He has placed me in such a position that I may find myself, any day, stranded without a husband and with one, or even with two, children. Everything to them is a joke, a momentary fancy. They get married, and like it, and produce a number of children, and then—drop it all and go off to fight. I ought to hope now that my child will die, for I will never survive him. I haven't much faith in all this patriotism and *enthousiasme* in a man of thirty-five.[46] Are not children the same *patrie*, the same Russia ? But no ! he is quite prepared to drop them because it's fine to gallop across the battlefield and revel in the romance of war and listen to the whistling of bullets ! His inconstancy and cowardice make me respect him less. His talent is almost more important to him than his family. Let him explain to me the important motives of his desire. Why did I ever get married to him ? Even Valerian Petrovich would have been preferable ; at least, I wouldn't have minded so much if he had left me. What did he need my love for ?

Was it merely a momentary infatuation ? I know it is my fault ; or why should he be so peevish ? It is my fault to love him and to be afraid of his absence and his death in the war. Let him be peevish : but I should like to have prepared myself for it by ceasing to love him, and then the parting would be easier. Let him push me away altogether, I also shall go further away from him. One year of happiness is enough for him ; and now he wants a change. He is tired of this life. He shan't have any more children ; I shan't give him any more, so that he can desert them. Just listen to the despot : " I want to do it, and don't you dare say a word." The war hasn't begun yet and he is still here. All the worse for me having to wait and languish. It will be the same in the end, anyway. And the worst of it is that I still love him. It breaks my heart to see him sad.

October 7.

I am very sad, but at least, my son gives me some joy. Why this nurse ? The everlasting fussing with the baby's clothes has at least helped to distract me. He notices my boredom, of course ; it's no good trying to hide it, but it'll be unbearable for him. I should like to go to the ball—but that isn't the cause of my boredom. I shan't go, of course, and it annoys me to think that I can still be tempted by it. This feeling would have spoiled all the fun, anyway—not that I would have really enjoyed it. He keeps saying : " I am being born anew." Why should he be ? Let him keep everything he had before his marriage, if only he can get rid of all this worry and restless longing to go hither and thither. " Born anew ? " He says :

"You will understand in time." But I feel lost, and don't seem to be able to understand him any longer. He seems to be undergoing some change. He and I are becoming more and more estranged. My illness and the baby have taken me away from him, and that must be why I have ceased to understand him. But what more can I want? Is it not happiness to have such an inexhaustible mind, so much talent, virtue, and thought, in one's husband? And yet I am bored. It's my *youth* . . .

October 17, 1863.

I can't understand him sufficiently, and that must be why I watch so jealously—his thoughts, his actions, his past and present. I should like to be able to grasp and understand him fully, so that he might treat me as he treated Alexandrine,[47] but I know that that is impossible, and I have to accept the fact that I am too young, too silly, and not sufficiently poetic. To be like Alexandrine, quite apart from any natural gifts, one needs to be older, childless, and possibly even unmarried. It wouldn't annoy me if they resumed their old correspondence, but it would hurt me to have her think that Lyova's wife was fit for nothing else except the nursery and commonplace everyday relations. But I am well aware that no matter how jealous I may be about his spirit, Alexandrine can not and must not be cut out of his life; she has played a part for which I would have been useless. I have been weeping because he didn't tell me all he had written, and because he had written: "Something that I alone know about myself. And I shall tell you this also, only my wife has nothing whatever to do with it." I should like to get to know her better. I wonder if she would think me worthy of him? She knew how to understand and to appreciate him. I found a letter from her inside the desk, and it made me ponder on her relation to Lyova. One of her letters is fine. I thought once or twice of writing to her, without mentioning it to Lyova, but I didn't dare. She interests me greatly, and I seem to like her very much. I have been thinking of her ever since I read Lyova's letter to her. I would have loved her. Judging by my frame of mind, I am not pregnant, and I hope this condition continues. I love him immensely, and it worries me to think that I will love him even more. I feel so happy, so peaceful, and so serene to-day, it is probably because he loves me these days. I don't believe he has deteriorated. I am waiting impatiently for his state of anxiety and his dissatisfaction with himself to pass away. It gives me joy to see an improvement in his frame of mind, and I am afraid of his present state. This mental strain eats away his life, which I need so much.

October 28, 1863.

I am feeling unhappy and depressed. As though our love were gone and nothing remained. He is calm and indifferent, working hard, but not cheerfully, while I feel angry and sad. Angry at myself, at my character, at my attitude towards my husband. As if I had promised him in my heart no more than this! My dear, dear Lyova! All the worry about the estate weighs heavily upon him—as if that were suitable work for him! May heaven forgive me my bad temper. I love him terribly much, but I feel lonely. I don't know how to be happy or to make others happy. My mental laziness appals me ; I feel disgusted with myself. If I am so helpless, then surely my love cannot be very strong. But no ! I love him terribly, terribly much. There can be no doubt about that. If only I could become myself again : my husband is so dear, so charming. What is he working on ? *The history of 1812.*[48] He used to tell me so much about his work, but now I seem to be unworthy of his confidence. In the past all his thoughts were mine. Those were wonderful, blissful moments : now they are gone. "Sonya, we shall always be happy." I am so sad because I realise that he doesn't get all the happiness he deserves and which he once expected.

November 13.

I feel sorry for Auntie : she won't last long. She is ill all the time now, and is unable to sleep at night because of her cough. Her hands are so thin and dry. I keep thinking about her all day long. He says he would like to live for a while in Moscow. I've been expecting it. It makes me jealous to see how he can find his ideal in the first pretty woman he meets. Such a passion is terrible, blind, and incurable. I have never lived up to his ideal, and never will. I feel abandoned during the day, in the evening, at night—all the time. I am a source of satisfaction to him, a nurse, a piece of furniture, *a woman*—nothing more. I try to suppress all human feelings in myself. While the machine works and warms the milk and knits a blanket and walks up and down without thinking, life is still bearable. He has stopped loving me. Why was I not able to keep his love ? But how could I ? It is Fate. There was a moment—I admit it—a moment of sorrow when nothing in the world mattered any more, except the love that I had lost. His writing meant nothing to me then—what did all those conversations matter between Countess So-and-so and Princess So-and-so ; but afterwards I despised myself for the thought. My existence is so deadly dull, while his is so full and rich, with his work and genius and immortal fame. I have begun to feel afraid of him, and at times I feel a complete stranger. But it is he who has placed me in such a position. It may be my own fault, for my temper has grown so much worse—and for some time now I have been feeling that I am no longer to him what I used to be. I take it patiently, thank heaven ; but I have become so full of apathy that nothing can excite or cheer me any longer. I don't know what is the matter with me, but I know that my instinct is right.

December 19, 1863.

I have lit two candles, and sat down at the table, and am now feeling quite happy. I am silly and a coward, but now I feel happy and lazy and free of care. Everything seems amusing and of no importance. I should like to flirt with somebody—I shouldn't even mind Alyosha Gorshok[41] —or lose my temper with a chair or anything at all. I played cards with Auntie for four solid hours ; it made him angry, but I didn't mind. It makes me terribly sad to think of Tanya. But I have put even that aside just now, such a silly mood has come over me. The child is better, *that* may be the reason I'm happy. At the moment I should love to go to a dance or do something amusing. Later

I shall blame myself for this mood, but I can't get away from it now. It annoys me to think how little Lyova cares, and how little he feels and understands how much I love him ; I should like to pay him back in his own coin. He is too old and solemn, while I feel full of youth and am longing to do something crazy. Instead of going to bed, I should like to turn somersaults. But with whom ?

December 24, 1863.

A feeling of old-age seems to have crept over me and everything around me is old. I try to suppress every feeling of youth, for it seems strange and out of place in such sedate, matter-of-fact surroundings. Serezha alone is younger in body and spirit than the others, and so I love to have him come here. I have gradually come to the conclusion that Lyova is a man who only *checks* me in everything. This restraint, which he imposes on me, also puts a check on any expression of love. How *can* one love when everything around is so quiet and sedate ? It is all so monotonous—especially when there is no love. I don't want to do anything. But I am grumbling as though I were really unhappy. But then I really *am* unhappy, for he doesn't love me much. So he told me, but then I knew it already. But I'm not sure about myself. I see so little of him, and am so afraid of him, that I don't really know how much I love him. I wanted to marry Tanya to Serezha, but I was frightened. What about Masha ——?[60] All Lyova's ideas about spiritual compartments are merely a result of his idealism, and are no consolation to me.

January 2, 1864.

Tanya, Tanya, Tanya. She is my only thought. I am tired of longing for things and of being sad. Lyova and Auntie and I—we are all in God's hands. But I feel very sad, and I wish they both could be very happy. I'm in a bad mood, I know. I was tired of Tula—such a dull place. I wanted to buy up the whole town—how silly !—but I was more reasonable in the end. Lyova was very sweet, and there was something childlike in his expression while he was playing. I remembered Alexandrine, and I could understand her feelings. I realised *how* she loved him. *Grandmother* was what he called her. He annoyed me just now by saying : " When you're in a bad mood, you always take to your diary." What does it matter to him, anyway ? I'm not in a bad mood just now. Every bit of sarcasm on his part hurts me terribly ; he should cherish my love better. I am so terribly afraid of being ugly—morally as well as physically.

March 27, 1864.

This diary is thickly covered with dust ; I haven't touched it for so long. And now, suddenly, I want to write down anything that comes into my head—surreptitiously, like a child. I am so anxious to love everybody and enjoy everything, but the moment anyone touches on this feeling everything falls to pieces. I was suddenly overcome with love and confidence in my husband ; but perhaps it was because it occurred to me that I might lose him. But to-day I made a firm resolution never, never to think of it again, and even to refuse to listen to him or to anybody else who would mention it. I love Tanya so well. Why are they spoiling her? But it's no good their attempting it, for they can never spoil her. I shall be very happy to have her here and shall take such care of her. I can at least be of great moral help to her—if nothing else. I shall keep her amused as much as I can. Tanya and Serezha[61] will be my children, and I'll take great care of them—it'll be fine. I believe that, compared to a year ago, I am less of an egoist now. My pregnancy had a very bad effect on me, and it annoyed me to think that I couldn't enjoy myself like other people. But now I am full of my own joy, and I am happier than anybody else.

April 22.

I am all alone. All day long I tried not to brood on my thoughts, but now that the evening has come I feel I must think it all over, and have a cry, and write everything down in my diary, although it might be far better to write to him—but that's impossible. But there's nothing to say : everything is dull and lifeless and monotonous. So long as little Serezha is with me, I manage to bear up, but after he is put to bed I begin to fuss and worry as if I had a thousand things to attend to ; but I really don't need anything and am simply trying to get away from my thoughts. I feel as if he were out shooting, or seeing about the beehives or the estate, and were coming in any moment. I am used to waiting, for he never comes back till I am just on the point of losing my temper. I wish I could think of something very unpleasant in our life, so that I might feel less sorry for him, but I can't do it, for the moment I think of him I realise how terribly I love him, and I want to cry. I sometimes catch myself thinking that I am *not* sad, and that makes me sad at once. To-day, for the first time in my life, I shall have to sleep entirely alone. They suggested that I should put Tanya's bed beside mine ; but I didn't want to. It must be Lyova or nobody. It would be easy for him to die, for he would know on his deathbed how faithful I would always be. But I am almost terrified at the thought of how much I trust him now. Am I not silly to be sitting here, swallowing my tears, as if I hadn't the right to weep because I feel lonely when my husband's away. I'll go on weeping like this for several days more. What if I do a silly thing and go to Nikolskoye ? I feel that, if I give enough vent to my tears, I'll be quite capable of doing it. This diary has upset me even more. What am I fit for, with so little endurance and will-power ? I don't want even to think of what he is doing now. I am sure he is happy and cheerful, and certainly not weeping like me. I am not ashamed, for I am alone and have almost stopped writing my diary. In any case, he never looks now to see if I have written anything. I am afraid to lie down, I am so weak-minded, and I'm sure that Tanya, who is in the drawing-room, will soon hear me cry, and I shall feel ashamed, especially after I have spent the day in such a sensible frame of mind.

November 3, 1864.

It's strange that amidst such happy surroundings I should have such a constant feeling of dread in case Lyova dies. This feeling grows stronger every day. Last night, and all the nights when I am sitting with my little girl, I feel so sad, so miserable at the thought that he may die, and I picture the scene of his death so clearly to myself. This feeling has been growing ever since the day on which he sprained his arm. I suddenly realised the possibility of losing him, and since then I've been thinking of nothing else. I am practically living in the nursery just now, nursing and looking after the children, and that distracts me. I often feel that this womanly world must bore him, and that I am incapable of making him happy ; I begin to believe that I am a good nurse—and nothing else. No brains, no education, no talent—nothing. I wish something would happen quickly, for I can feel it coming. Looking after the children, playing with Serezha—all this keeps me amused at times, and yet there is nothing in which I can take *real* joy ; all my old cheerfulness seems to have disappeared. Often before have I known that some misfortune would come, such as Lyova's irritation against me. For all I know, he may be secretly hating me.

February 25, 1865.

I am so often left alone with my thoughts that the desire to write my diary is quite natural. I sometimes feel depressed, but now it seems wonderful to be able to think everything over for myself, without having to say anything about it to other people. It's extraordinary how many different thoughts run through my head. Yesterday Lyova said that he was feeling very young ; and I understood him perfectly. Now I am well once again, and not pregnant ; it terrifies me to think how often I have been in that condition. He said that youth meant the capacity to say: "*I can accomplish everything.*" As for me, I both *can* and *want* to do everything, but after a while I begin to realise that there is nothing to want, and that I can't do anything beyond eating, drinking, sleeping, nursing the children, and caring for them and my husband. After all, that *is* happiness, yet why do I grow sad and weep, as I did yesterday? I am writing with a feeling of pleasant excitement, for I know that no one, not even Lyova, will read this, and that is why I can be perfectly candid in all I say. He has gone out; he doesn't spend much time with me these days.

When I am *young* I prefer not to be with him; for I fear to be stupid and irritable. Dunyasha said the other day: "The count has grown old." I wonder if it is true. He is never gay now, and I often seem to get on his nerves; his writing takes up much of his time, but gives him no pleasure. I wonder if he has lost for ever his capacity to be happy and joyful? He is talking of spending next winter in Moscow. He will probably be happier in Moscow, and I shall pretend that I also want to be there. I have never admitted to him that unconsciously, in order to rise in his estimation, one can be a hypocrite even with one's own husband. I did not tell him that, for I am petty and vain, and even envious of people. But I shall be ashamed in Moscow not to have a carriage and pair, with a footman in livery, and fine dresses and a fine house, and everything in general. Lyova is extraordinary—he simply doesn't care about such things. It's a result of his wisdom and his virtue.

My children are my greatest happiness. When I am alone, I feel disgusted with myself, but the children make me feel good. I prayed over Tanya yesterday, yet now I can hardly understand why and how one ought to pray. When I am with my children I stop feeling *young*, but I feel happy and serene.

March 6, 1865.

Serezha is ill. I seem to be wandering about as in a dream—nothing real, only hazy impressions, and a dim capacity of knowing whether he is better or worse. Lyova is young and full of strength and energy, busy working, in his independent way. I can feel that he is strength and life itself, while I am only a worm crawling and feeding on him. I am afraid of being weak; after my illness, my nerves are in a bad state, and I'm so ashamed of it. The last *cut* I received from Lyova is still hurting me. I am waiting, almost with a feeling of guilt, and yet I am afraid to wait—for what if his affection never again returns? I regard him with a feeling of veneration, yet I have fallen so low myself; I know it, for else why should I always want to point out his weak spots? This evening everything seemed so strange. He went out, and I stayed here, and everything around me was silent. The children are fast asleep. The rooms upstairs are so fresh and clean and empty that those gaudy flowers and their strong perfume seem strangely out of place; I am almost frightened of the sound of my footsteps and I am even afraid to breathe. Lyova came in for a moment and everything at once became cheerful and bright. He seemed to bring in with him the smell of fresh air, and to me he seems like fresh air itself.

March 8, 1865.

Everything has become so gay and happy. Serezha is better ; his illness is over. Lyova is very cheerful, though he is still cold and indifferent to me. I'm afraid to say he *doesn't love me*, but the thought of it keeps torturing me, and my hesitation makes me shy in his presence. I felt terribly depressed during the sorrowful days when Serezha was so ill. I do not accept misfortunes patiently—that is bad. My head was full of dreadful ideas ; it would be shameful to admit them. As Lyova was very cool to me and often went out, I began to wonder whether he was seeing A——. This thought kept tormenting me all day long ; Serezha, however, distracted me to a certain extent, and, now that I come to think of it, it makes me feel ashamed. I should know him better by now. If it were true, he couldn't be so calm and natural and sincere with me. But there's no getting away from it—as long as she and I are in this place, I simply cannot help thinking of it each time Lyova is cold to me, or I am in a bad mood. But what if he were suddenly to come back and tell me . . . but no, this is frightful nonsense, I'm ashamed of it, and ought to confess this evil thought which, though only in a dim, vague manner, has come into my mind.

March 9, 1865.

Lyova is still very cool to me. I have a cold in my head and am feeling disgusting and miserable. I am silent all day long, brooding over my thoughts and looking through the window at the beauty of Nature, and rejoicing in the coming of spring. The children have colds, too, and are coughing, and Serezha is looking so thin and miserable. I love my children so much that I am almost afraid of expressing my love in a commonplace way. Lyova is killing me with his indifference and lack of interest. He only expects me to be interested in all he does, as if he didn't know how much I love it all. I am feeling calm and even subdued—a mood that only seldom comes to me. I keep thinking of my mother and sisters. Lyova can't understand my love for my parents. I am longing to see them. It seems to me that I annoy Lyova each time I mention going to Moscow. He only thinks of his own advantages in going to Moscow, and never has any desire to give me some pleasure. I wonder if I am selfish, but I don't think I am. I would do anything in the world for Lyova. He once said that I had no will-power ; perhaps it is just as well. I shall be able to submit to any circumstances without longing for something different. But I don't want to be weak-minded, and am doing a great deal just now. Lyova is out shooting, while I have been busy copying all morning. I shall be glad to see Auntie again, for I am very fond of her ; but, all the same, it'll spoil the solitude to which I have got used, and which I am beginning to like, for it alone lets me feel quite free and sincere with myself. I am afraid of Lyova. He has begun to notice all my bad points. I'm coming to believe that there is very little good in me.

March 10, 1865.

Lyova has a headache. He has gone on horseback to Yasenki. I am unwell most of the time, too, and the children are miserable with their coughs and colds. I simply don't know what can be done to improve

Serezha's health. He is terribly thin, doesn't eat, seems to be dull, and is constantly suffering from diarrhœa. I have just received a letter from Auntie ; she was greatly touched by my letter ; she is ill, and has a cough. I feel a " gentle hatred " for Mashenka, as Lyova would say, but I have a real affection for her children, though with a certain degree of condescension. Lyova is becoming more affectionate. He kissed me to-day, and that hasn't happened for a long time. But it was all poisoned by the thought that he hasn't l—— with me for such a long time. I do a great deal of copying for him, and am glad to be of use to him in some way.

March 14, 1865.

I have a terrible headache these days, but I feel very energetic in the evenings, wanting to do all kinds of things and enjoy life to the utmost. Lyova is playing Chopin's " Preludes." He is in a very good state of mind, though he is still cold towards me. My children take up all my thoughts. Both are suffering from diarrhœa, which drives me quite frantic. Dyakov has been here ; he's as much of a nightingale as ever, as Tanya says—never stops talking. I like him, he's a nice, simple man. There are no signs of spring yet ; it's still bitterly cold. I am much concerned about the weather—it's of importance both to the children and to my frame of mind. I am waiting for the spring as if for a blessing, and it is late in coming this year. Lyova often wants to go to Tula ; he seems to need more company nowadays. Sometimes I feel the same way, not about company in general, but I should love to see Tanya and the Zephyrotes,[11] and Father and Mother.

March 15, 1865.

Lyova has gone to Tula: I am glad. Serezha's child is dying, and it is making me feel terribly sad. My headache is much better and I am feeling well and full of energy. The children aren't very well yet, although they are much better. The sun came out for a moment and it affected me as much as a waltz affects a girl of sixteen. I am longing for the spring and the summer and country walks. I haven't had any letters from the family for a long time. I wonder how my pretty, poetic Tanya is? My relations with Lyova are good and simple; he says he has been greatly dissatisfied with himself these days. I love him terribly, and simply couldn't deteriorate with a man like him. His knowledge of himself and his confession makes me feel very humble, and compels me to notice every little bit of evil in myself.

March 16, 1865.

I have a terrible headache; the children are in indifferent health. Serezha had a temperature to-day. I can't understand what is wrong with him. Lyova has been out of doors all day long. Where is he? What is he doing? I got a letter from Tanya yesterday, which came with her luggage. I am so glad to think of seeing her so soon, and it was like meeting an old friend to come across some of my old girlish dresses among her things. Serezha's son has died. I was so sorry that I wept this morning. My headache keeps me from doing any work, and my nerves are all on edge.

March 20, 1865.

I've been feeling feverish for two mornings now and have a terrible headache. I feel like a mangy dog in front of Lyova, and don't disturb him, although, in any case, he pays no attention to me. I'm sad to think that I don't exist for him, and yet I feel as jealous as ever. I am spoilt. As I was reading to-day an article on the *Cossacks*, and recalling the novel to my mind, I again realised so clearly that I was the borderline which divided him from all the life and love and youth that belonged to the Cossack girls and other women. I have become terribly attached to the children, and have devoted myself to them completely. I feel they need me, and that gives me great happiness. When I nurse Tanya, or when Serezha puts his little arms firmly round my neck, I feel no jealousy, no sorrow, no regret, no desire for anything more—nothing. Now they are both ill, and nothing can make me happy. It's lovely spring weather outside, but I shall never again be able to get full enjoyment out of nature. I keep on admiring Lyova : he is so happy, so strong in body and in mind. It is terrible to feel so humble ; the one armour that can put me on a basis of equality with him is my energy, my youth, my children, and the fact that I am a good and healthy wife. But at present I am still only a mangy dog.

March 23.

My fever has gone, and with it my depression. I am greatly perturbed, for the children are still not well. Lyova has gone to Tula to get a doctor. Our relations are very good. I feel happy and free with him and am no longer troubled with doubts and jealousy. The weather is lovely. Spring has come, and the brooks are rustling, and yet I am indoors. Lyova is very busy with the dairy farm, and the novel isn't making very much progress at present. His head is bursting with ideas—but when will he ever write them down? He sometimes speaks to me of his plans and ideas, which is always a joy to me, and I can always follow him. But what am I talking about? I shan't write down his conversation, anyway.

March 26.

I have been tidying the rooms in a fit of "orderliness"; I always feel like that after putting Serezha and Tanya to bed. They are nearly quite well now. Tanya sometimes makes me tremble with fright. The fear of death, this constant misfortune of all living beings, has started troubling me again. Lyova is in an irritable mood, and, in spite of myself, sometimes annoys me. A terrible thought: What if, after taking so little notice of me, and taking my love so much for granted, he suddenly discovered that I had become indifferent towards him? But that is impossible, and that is why it is so easy to speak of it; he knows it, and so he will always value me less than he should. Serezha has spent a few days with us. He is very pitiful, and I am beginning to get quite fond of him. He makes me feel at ease. It is a dull, cloudy spring; but I am again feeling the old childish thrill at the approach of Easter. To-morrow is Palm Saturday, a day I always loved in my girlhood. After that comes Holy Saturday, which isn't any different from any other week-day during Lent. I am much calmer now; in the past I used to weep so often. Yesterday Serezha said : " There is nothing good in the world except love and the moon, and music and the nightingales." We talked about it, and I didn't feel in the least shy ; but when I speak to Lyova, he always looks at me as if he were saying : " What right have you to discuss these things. You are unable to feel them anyway." Sometimes, indeed, I don't *dare* to feel them. Lyova likes a lonely, poetic existence ; there must be so much fine poetry in him which he keeps all to himself. That has taught me, also, to have a separate little life of my own. I can hear him writing something ; it must be his diary, too. I hardly ever read it nowadays, for if you know that anyone is going to read your diary you stop being sincere in what you write. As for me, I have become much more sincere lately, and my life seems to have become very bright and pleasant. He also writes down the new ideas for his novel—it is all so *clever*, and my empty-headedness always terrifies me when I am with him.

April 1.

Lyova is in Tula, and I am feeling quite desperate. For he has been complaining about his health—his blood-pressure and indigestion and noises in his head, and all this worries me a great deal, and I feel it even more when I am sitting here all alone, in this warm, glorious spring weather. Both the children are nearly well, and I have taken them out, so that now for the first time in her six months' existence Tanya has seen God's beautiful world. I have been doing nothing all day long except trying to get away from my gloomy thoughts. He says that physical unfitness takes half your life away. And yet his life is so necessary. I love him so deeply, and it annoys me to think how little I can do to make him completely happy. I have no evil feelings of any kind towards him, only love which is so immense that it almost terrifies me.

May 3.

A bad spring. Tanya has arrived, and they are all busy shooting and riding. I am on excellent terms with everybody and we are all very well, and yet everything seems to have turned topsy-turvy. I have been quarrelling with Lyova. I am still spiteful and untamed, but I shall improve in time. The children are ill. I am angry with Tanya for poking her nose too much into Lyova's life. He keeps going to Nikolskoye, shooting, riding, or walking. My jealousy burst out yesterday for the first time, and now it makes me sad to think of it. I have given her my horse, which I think is very good of me. It is so easy to approve of one's own actions. The two of them have gone together to the wood. I get the strangest ideas into my head.

June 9, 1865.

Everything was settled the other day between Tanya and Serezha. They are going to be married. It's a joy to look at them, and their happiness gives me more pleasure than my own ever did. As they walked about the garden, I acted chaperon, which both amused and annoyed me. Serezha is very nice to me now on account of Tanya ; and everything is going to be splendid. The wedding is to be in twenty days or so. I wonder how it'll turn out ? She has loved him for a long time ; she is charming and has a sweet character ;

I'm glad to think that we shall be even greater friends. The weather is bad : Lyova and Tanya have colds, and Serezha, Grisha, and Keller[53] have gone to Pirogovo.[54] It's been a dull day ever since morning. It's depressing having to wait for anything ; I shall be so glad to see them happily married. We shall soon go to Nikolskoye, where the wedding is to take place ; I've been reading her diary to-day. It was so sad to read of all her past sorrows and sufferings that I often stopped, nearly in tears ; but she thought that I was merely bored and didn't want to go on reading it. Lyova isn't very cheerful these days ; the children are charming, and are making great progress.

Nikolskoye, July 12, 1865.

It has all fallen through : Serezha has deceived Tanya. He has behaved like a perfect cad. It's now a whole month since it happened, and it breaks my heart to look at Tanya. To think that such a charming, poetic, and talented girl should be wasted like this. Her symptoms of consumption worry me terribly. I shall never be able to give a really full account of all this sad story. My anger at Serezha is boundless, and if ever I have a chance of revenge I shall take it. Tanya's attitude to the whole affair was very noble. She loved him very much, while he only pretended. The gipsy woman was dearer to him.[17] But Masha is a good woman ; I feel sorry for her and have really nothing against her ; but he is certainly revolting. "Just wait a little, wait a little," he kept on saying, and at the same time was just deceiving her and only playing about with her emotions. In the end Tanya couldn't stand it any longer ; she realised the ridiculous part she was playing, and, feeling sorry both for him, whom she still loved, and for Masha and her children, she broke off the engagement. They had been engaged for twelve days, and he had kissed her and talked the usual platitudes, building up plans for the future and what not—an utter cad. I shall tell everybody about it, and let my children know it, too—it'll teach them not to behave like him. My own family life at home is calm, happy, and serene. Why have I deserved so much happiness? Both the children and Lyova are well, and we are most affectionate to one another ; the summer weather is gloriously warm, and everything is just wonderful. If only this miserable business hadn't disturbed our quiet, honourable life. We have been in Nikolskoye ever since June 28, Serezha's birthday. We have had some visitors already—the Dyakovs and Mashenka,[55] with her daughters, and yesterday dear old Dyakov came again, and did much to cheer Tanya up. In the morning, Volkov, a neighbour of ours, came here for the first time. A timid, gentle kind of man, with fair hair and a turned-up nose. I rather liked him. Life here is full of variety : the river, and bathing, the hills and the heat, and contented minds, red berries and Tanya's grief. The children are a great joy to me, and my dear Lyova is in a most happy and poetic mood. I am happy, too : but how long will it last?

July 16.

I had a row with Nurse ; she is such a good woman, and I feel thoroughly ashamed of myself. I tried to put things right, and nearly apologised to her, only it's no good getting sentimental with these people—they don't understand it, anyway. The Fets[11] are staying with us ; they are pleasant enough people, though he is a little on the pompous side, while she is rather plain, but a very good woman for all that. Poor Tanya is upsetting me terribly. She is in a terrible state of inertia, and the fear of consumption is hanging over her. Little Tanya was ill, and I was greatly worried, but now she is better. She is such a nice, lively little thing, and her eyes and her smile are a joy to me. Serezha often cries ; it must be the result of his illness, but, apart from that, he is very sweet and gentle. The thunderstorm to-day made me very nervous. Lyova keeps reading the war scenes in his novel ; I don't care much for those parts.

Why did I quarrel with Nurse ? I am very like my mother, and it grieves me to find in myself the traits which I always disliked in her. Especially the conviction that I am a good woman, and that therefore all my weaknesses ought to be forgiven me. I really want to be good, and to be fully alive to my faults, nor do I want anyone to overlook them, least of all myself. I've quite made up my mind about it.

October 26, 1865.

It is cheerful to take up the diary again, probably because I love myself and the whole life within me. Why is it regarded as a general rule that husbands, who are in love with you, at first, should always grow cold as time goes on ? I have made the discovery that a woman does not really become *genuine* until she has been married for some years, and if one in a million does not change as a result of marriage, and still remains as sweet and charming as before, her husband (provided he, too, is a good one) will be sure to remain in love with her all his life. I have changed immensely ; I wonder if I have ever pretended ? I am much, much worse than I was, and Lyova's coldness has stopped affecting me, for I know that I deserve it. It no longer drives me to tears or despair, as it once did ; in those days I was much kinder and more meek and gentle. Now for a short account. We have been in Yasnaya since October 12. Tanya is staying with the Dyakovs. She is in poor health, and I shudder to think of losing her. Lyova has been unwell, but now he is better and is busy writing. The children are well, and I want to stop nursing the baby—though the thought of it makes me very sad. Lyova has taught me to ascribe everything to physical causes ; it's very unpleasant, and yet I am gradually beginning to see things in the same light. Auntie is in very good health and is so pitiful. I am too cold to her. Haven't I a drop of affection left in me ? I believe I am pregnant, but that gives me no joy. I am afraid of everything and feel unfriendly towards the whole world. It's a strange desire for power, for being above everybody else. It is hard even for me to understand, and yet it is true.

March 12, 1866.

We spent six weeks in Moscow, and returned here on the seventh, and Yasnaya Polyana once again filled me with a sense of calm, and slightly wistful happiness. I liked Moscow, for I love my people so much, and they were all so delighted with my children. Tanya is a bright, clever, and healthy little thing. Serezha is much stronger now and a little less gentle than he was before, but a nice reasonable little fellow. I'm afraid of being partial in judging my children, but I am really very pleased with them, and they make me very happy indeed. My relations with Lyova were somewhat cool and strained during our Moscow visit; P.'s coarse behaviour, following on my inability to adopt the right attitude towards him, somewhat spoiled the relations between us.

I feel disgusted and ashamed, and yet there isn't a stain on my conscience in all my years of married life, and Lyova really judged me a little too harshly in that matter. But, at any rate, it shows that he treasures me, and I shall only be too delighted to be a hundred times more careful in future. Still, I am terrified of every new *cut*. I have to humble myself all the time, which always means a loss in that pleasant sense of pride and dignity without which I could not live. In Moscow we spent most of the time with my people. In the morning the coach would come for the children, and we would go off to the Kremlin. Lyova kept going to his sculpture classes and to the gymnasium. Of all our friends, the people we saw most of were the Perfilievs, the Bashilovs, and Princess Gorchakov; we also got to know Princess Obolensky. I used to go to concerts, and developed a great liking for classical music. Everything went well, and I came to love everything in Moscow, even our Dmitrovka Street and our stuffy bed-sitting room, and the study where Lyova was busy modelling a red horse, and where we had so many talks in the evening. Petya is a darling, and I grew very fond of him. When I think about them all I feel sad not to be seeing them any more.

March 22.

In the years of youth, one's impression of life are unconscious and spontaneous ; that is what makes them so valuable ; they are also far more plentiful than in later life, when one is over-inclined to ponder only on the more serious experiences. It is much less cheerful.

April 28.

When men get married they imagine that they are taking such-and-such a girl with such-and-such a character, etc., and they don't seem to realise that everything will change, and that it is no good saying "I am happy" until after the old mechanism has gradually been replaced by the new one. The important factor here is not so much the girl's character, but all the influences which she undergoes during the early stages of her married life. Everybody is envying us our happiness, and this makes me wonder why we are so happy and what it all means.

June 9, 1866.

Our son Ilya was unexpectedly born on May 22. I didn't think it would happen until the middle of June.

July 19.

We've got a new factor for the estate. His wife is young, good-looking, and a *nihilist*. She and Lyova have long, lively talks on literature and politics. I find these talks rather out of place—flattering to her, and painful to me. He used to preach that an outsider, especially a young and attractive person, ought not to be admitted into the intimate family circle—and yet in practice he always does the opposite. Of course, I don't show any sign of being displeased, although I haven't a moment of peace now. Since Ilya's birth we have been sleeping in separate rooms, which is wrong ; for if we were together I wouldn't stand it any longer, but would blurt it all out to him this very evening ; but I can't go to him now,—and it is the same with him. My children make me very happy ; they give me so much joy that it seems a sin to ask for more. There is so much happiness in loving them ; but it is a pity that Lyova should break his own rules. Yet why did he say to-day that a husband would be afraid to hurt a wife, whose conduct was irreproachable ? As if one were only unhappy after one's husband had already *done* something evil. It's a great enough misfortune if for a second one's husband doubts in his soul that he loves his wife. Lyova is wrong to treat Marya Ivanovna to such grand speeches. It is nearly one o'clock, but I can't sleep. I just feel as if that nihilist woman was going to be my *bête noire*.

July 22, 1866.

This morning Lyova made some excuse for going to *that* house. So M. I. told me, and she also said that he had talked to her below her balcony. What was the need of going there in the rain ? It's quite obvious that he likes her, and the thought of it drives me insane. I wish her every misfortune, but to her face, for some reason, I am particularly pleasant. I wonder how soon her husband will turn out to be useless, so that they can both go away ? But, in the meantime, this jealousy will kill me. He is extremely cold to me. My breasts are very sore, and it is real agony to nurse the child. I called in Marfusha to-day, and made her feed the child, so that my breasts might have a rest. My suffering always seems to make him treat me badly ; he always grows cold, and that adds mental agony to my physical pain. I remain locked up in my own room, while she sits in the drawing-room with the children. I simply can't bear her ; it annoys me to see her beauty and vivaciousness, especially when Lyova is there.

July 24.

Lyova went again to that house, and said afterwards that the poor woman found life very dull. Then he asked me why I hadn't invited them to dinner. If only I could forbid her ever to come into the house at all, I would gladly do it. My dear Lyova ! Can't you see how easily you get caught ! The pain in my breasts takes up much of my time and happiness. The worst of it is that Lyova and I have become strangers to one another. I got Marfusha to nurse Ilyusha, who is rather restless ; and it makes me sad to see him suck somebody else's breast. Goodness only knows when my breasts will heal ; everything seems to be all wrong. My heart leaps with joy when I see Lyova dissatisfied with the farm work. Maybe he'll dismiss the factor, and then I'll get rid of this dreadful feeling of jealousy. I'd be sorry for him, but I cannot bear her.

August 10, 1866.

There are days when I feel so happy and cheerful that I long to do something which would make everybody love and admire me. In contrast to the misfortunes of which I have heard, I feel particularly happy. Bibikov told us a terrible story yesterday, about a regimental clerk in Yasenky who was shot for hitting his lieutenant in the face. Lyova defended him at the open court-martial, but, unfortunately, the defence was a purely formal affair. I learned to-day of the death of Constance's little son, and felt so sorry for her.

We have had lots of visitors ; the Gorchakov princesses, Prince Lvov, a very nice man, and that fat fellow Sollogub,[67] with his two sons. He said that I was the ideal " author's wife "—one who knew how to *nurse her husband's talent ;* I am grateful to him for saying it, and shall do my best to be even more of a nurse for Lyova's talent. My jealousy about M. I. has completely gone—there was really nothing in it. My relations with Lyova are good and pleasant, though still a little cold. My children are such darlings. Serezha started calling me *thou* to-day. I am sorry to find that he has forgotten his alphabet during the summer ; last winter he knew it so well.

August 27.

I love my children passionately, almost painfully ; their slightest pain drives me to despair, and every little smile brings tears to my eyes. Ilyusha is unwell ; I'm expecting the Dyakovs, Tanya, and Masha, with her girls. They are going to stay in the new house, where the rooms have already been got ready for them. Nursing is certainly hard work, and it often makes me quite weak. It would be easier if I didn't love the children so much.

November 12.

Lyova has taken Tanya to Moscow. Her health is very bad, and this is worrying me dreadfully. I love her intensely, and the more hopeless her health becomes the greater is my attachment to her. She will probably go with the Dyakovs to Italy. I didn't notice anything much wrong with her during the autumn. We were all so happy during the first three weeks in September that I instinctively suppressed all unhappy thoughts. When I don't write in my diary for a long time, I always feel sorry that I have not said anything about how happy I have been in the interval. The Dyakovs, Mashenka, with her girls, and Tanya spent those three weeks with us, and my relations with Tanya were so intimate, so friendly, and natural, that it would be hard to find the like of it. It gives me joy to think of my name-day (on September 17), when at dinner, much to my pleasant surprise, the band began to play.[58] I remember the affectionate look in Lyova's eyes during that day, and the evening we spent on the verandah, which was lit up with Chinese lanterns, and I can still see the gay young girls in their white muslin dresses, and that genial little fellow, Kolokoltsev, and, above all, my beloved Lyova, looking so lively and excited, and doing his best to make us as happy as possible. I was surprised that such a sedate and solemn matron as myself could dance with so much gusto. The weather was glorious, and everything was lovely. After the visitors had gone, Tanya stayed on with us for another month, and during that time her bad health became obvious. Especially now that Lyova is gone, I am feeling terribly upset about her. Lyova's absence always makes me sad. I don't believe two people could be spiritually more intimate than we are. How extremely fortunate we are in every way—our friendship, our children, our life generally. Now that he is away, I give even more of my life to the children, only they are still so little. Now they are sleeping, then they'll eat, then they'll sleep again, but, at the same time, I try to catch and enjoy every little expression of their *minds.* I spend a great deal of time copying out Lyova's novel (without reading it previously). This is a very great pleasure to me. As I copy it, I live through a whole new world of ideas and impressions. Nothing has such an effect on me as his ideas and his genius. This is something quite new with me. Have I changed a great deal, or is it because the novel is so extraordinarily good? I don't know. I copy at a great speed, and so am able to follow the gist of the story, and yet at the same time the copying is sufficiently slow to allow me to feel and to ponder over each new idea. We often discuss the novel, and I am very proud to say that he pays a great deal of attention to any remarks I make.

January 12, 1867.

I am in a terrible state of worry and distraction, just as though something were coming to an end. So many things are bound to come to an end, and the thought terrifies me. The children have been ill all this time, and I still can't get used to the English nurse and still feel unfriendly towards her. I believe one always feels very depressed before dying. I am fussed and worried, and seem to be in a constant hurry to do things. All this winter Lyova kept on writing, full of irritation and excitement, and with tears coming to his eyes. I believe his novel is going to be wonderful. The parts he reads to me often bring tears into my eyes; is it because I am his wife and can sympathise with him, or is the novel really so wonderful? I believe it is the latter. His family gets only his *fatigues de travail*, and he has become impatient and irritable with me, so that I am beginning to feel very lonely.

March 15, 1867.

A fire broke out at the hothouse at ten o'clock last night and burnt it to the ground. I was in bed when it started, and when Lyova wakened me we could see a bright glare from our window. Lyova was busy getting the gardener's children and his furniture out of the house, while I ran to the village for help. But it was useless, and everything was destroyed—even the plants that Lyova's grandfather had planted, and which had gladdened the heart of three generations; and the little that was left must be damaged by the fire and the frost. I didn't feel so upset about it last night, but to-day I have been trying all the time to keep back my tears. It's terribly sad, and, above all, I feel so sorry for Lyova; it has upset him very much, and every sorrow of his weighs heavily on my mind. He used to give so much time and attention to all those plants and flowers, many of which he had planted himself. But it can't be helped, and time alone will help us to forget it.

August 29.

We have been quarrelling, and haven't got over it yet. "It's your own fault if you haven't learned what your husband likes and what he can tolerate." All the time we were quarrelling I kept saying to myself: "may it end speedily and well." And yet it kept going from bad to worse. It is a painful struggle seeking for the truth ; but none of my intentions were evil, I know it. Nothing is left to me now but jealousy, and fear and the memory of what is lost for ever.

September 12.

Yes, it has all gone. Everything seems so cold and unfriendly, and I feel I have lost all his love and candour. This feeling keeps pursuing me. I fear to be left alone, and yet I fear to be with him. I give a start every time he begins to speak, in case he says I repel him. But he says nothing, and doesn't lose his temper, although he doesn't love me any longer and never refers to our relations. I never dreamed it could come to this ; and it is all so unbearably sad. At times I am filled with proud anger, and then I feel I can do without his love, seeing he hasn't learned to love a woman like *me* ; but most of all it irritates me to think that I still love him so deeply and painfully and with such humility. Mother often boasts that Father has loved her all this time ; but it required no skill on her part ; it was simply because he knew how to love, which is a special gift. How can one *attach* anyone to one's self? There is no way. I have always been told that a woman must love her husband and be honourable and be a good wife and mother. They write such things in A B C books, and it is all nonsense. The thing to do is *not* to love, to be clever and sly, and to hide all one's bad points—as if anyone in the world had no faults ! And the main thing is *not* to love. See what

I have done by loving him so deeply ! And what can I do now with all my love ? It is so painful and humiliating ; but he thinks that it is merely silly. "You say one thing and always do another." But what is the good of arguing in this superior manner, when I have nothing in me but this humiliating love and a bad temper ; and these two things have been the cause of all my misfortunes, for my temper has always interfered with my love. I want nothing but his love and sympathy, and he won't give it me ; and all my pride is trampled in the mud ; I am nothing but a miserable, crushed worm, whom no one wants, whom no one loves, a useless creature with morning sickness, and a big belly, two rotten teeth, and a bad temper, a battered sense of dignity, and a love which nobody wants and which nearly drives me insane.

September 14.

It is still the same, and I am beginning to believe that one can endure anything, and still go on living ; it is a kind of calm, subdued, poetic existence, without excitements, without any of the things called physical and material ; a life full of holy thoughts and prayers, with a love that has been trampled on, and with nothing but the constant aim of self-perfection. Let no one, not even Lyova, approach this spiritual world of mine, let no one love me, and yet I shall love them all, and be happier and stronger than anyone else.

September 16, 1867.

In spite of myself, I keep thinking of the 17th of September a year ago. Heaven knows, I want no music, no dancing, none of all that, but merely his desire to give me pleasure and to see me happy as then ; if only he knew how grateful I still am, and always will be, for his kind thought last year. I firmly believed then that I was happy and strong and beautiful, and now I only feel that he doesn't love me, and that I am a weak, ugly, useless woman. He talked about the estate this morning, and we discussed things in such a friendly way, as though we were *one* again ; we so seldom talk to each other at all nowadays. My children and my own miserable thoughts make up my whole life. Just now Serezha came up to me and said : " What are you writing in your little book ? " I told him that when he grew up he would be allowed to read it. I wonder what he'll think, and how he will judge me ? I wonder if my children will also stop loving me ? I expect to be loved, and yet I find it so difficult to make people love me.

July 31, 1868.

It makes me laugh to read over this diary. It's so full of contradictions, and one would think I was such an unhappy woman. Yet is there a happier woman than I ? It would be hard to find a happier or more friendly marriage than ours. Sometimes, when I am alone in the room, I just laugh with joy, and making the sign of the cross, say to myself, ' May God let this last many, many years.' I always write in my diary when we quarrel. We still quarrel, sometimes, but only on account of some very subtle psychological differences, which we wouldn't even notice if we didn't love one another so much. I shall soon have been married for six years, and I still love him more and more. He often says that this is not really love, but merely a habit, and that we couldn't do without each other now. And yet I still love him in the same restless, passionate, jealous, and poetic way, and at times his placid ways annoy me.

He has gone out shooting with Petya. He is unable to write much in the summer. Later, they will go on to Nikolskoye. I am not feeling well and am staying in the house all day. The children are out all the time, and only come in to have their meals on the verandah. Little Ilya is a joy. Tanya is entirely taken up with Dasha[59] and rarely comes to see me, except for a moment. Kuzminsky seems to be neither fish nor flesh.

June 5, 1870.

I stopped nursing little Lyova four days ago. I felt almost sorrier for him than for any of the others. I blessed him as I took leave of him, and cried and prayed ; this first complete separation from one's child is very painful indeed. I must be pregnant again. With each child one gives away a part of one's own life and bends down afresh with the weight of so much illness, anxiety, and long years of responsibility.

August 18, 1871.

Last night I saw Tanya and her children off to the Caucasus,[60] and I am feeling sad and melancholy at the thought of being separated from such a dear friend. We have never been separated before, and it seems as if a bit of my soul had been torn away, leaving no consolation of any kind. There is no other human being who can infuse so much new life into me, who can console me so well in my sorrow and cheer me up when I am depressed. As I look at Nature and at my whole future, it all seems dead and hopeless without Tanya. I have no words to express my feelings. Something has died within me ; it is a sorrow that one cannot weep away all at once, for it will linger on for years and add pain to every memory of the past. I have the same feeling of anxiety about Lyova's health. The two-month *kumiss*[61] cure has done him no good ; the disease is still in him ; I can't see it, but I can feel it as I watch that strange apathy towards life and his surroundings, which began to show itself last winter. A shadow seems to have passed between us, and divided us. I know that unless I rise spiritually, i.e., get over the effect of Tanya's departure, and take a new interest in my children, without letting myself be bored or sad, even he will be unable to restore me to my old frame of mind ; for I feel him dragging me into the sad and hopeless atmosphere which seems to surround him. He does not admit this hopelessness himself, but my instincts never betray me. It is I who suffer most from his bad moods, and so I know.

Last winter, when both Lyova and I were so ill, something seemed to break in our lives. I lost my strong faith in life and happiness. I lost some of my strength of mind, and am now constantly obsessed with the fear that something will happen. And things *do* happen. Tanya has gone and Lyova is ill—the two human beings I love more than anything in the world. I have lost them both—Lyova because he is no longer the same as he used to be. He calls it " old age," but

I call it "illness." But this *something*, whatever it is, has come between us.

1872.

This winter has been a happy one ; we have been so intimate, and Lyova's health has not been bad.

[*March 30.*]

On March 30 Lyova came back from Moscow. The children have been bringing yellow and purple flowers into the house.

April 1, 1872.

I have been fasting. Returned from Tula by train, then by carriage ; there is snow only in the ravines, terrible mud, but the weather is warm and clear. Lyova went shooting in the evening, and shot a snipe. Mitrofan sent another.

April 3.

Still warm. He shot two snipe. We were sending off the proofs of the A B C, stayed up working till four in the morning.

April 5.

He shot another snipe ; took the children to see the beehives before dinner, but we couldn't cross the ford ; so I came back and walked about near the house with little Lyova. Very warm and a warm wind.

6.

A bright, windy morning ; but later a violent hail storm. Lyova has been unwell and feverish for the past three nights.

8.

Terrific thunderstorm and rain during the night. Lyova keeps feeling chilly and unwell. He is in good spirits, and says he has enough work to last him an endless number of years. Everything is green ; the leaves are coming out, and the grass is quite high already.

April 9.

Just like summer.

April 12.

We went out to the woods, and took little Ilya with us. A lovely still evening. We enjoyed it immensely. A full moon was rising over the tree-tops.

16.

Easter Sunday. Rain and thunder last night. Cold and dull in the morning.

18.

L. went shooting with Bibikov. Shot three in the Zaseka wood. Still cold.

19.

All night, till dawn, Lyova kept looking at the stars.

20.

I went with Varya and the children to pick violets. I am feeling a little feverish. Lyova is well. In the evening Varya's fiancé arrived.

21.

The children and I went out to gather mushrooms with Varya and Nagorny.[11] We got a whole basketful.

It is still cool. Lyova went out shooting, and Varya and her fiancé went with him. The setting sun was like a bright-red ball of fire. It's a quiet, warm evening, eleven degrees above zero. The lime-trees are opening up, and all the other trees, except the oaks, are in leaf. This morning, Lyova brought in a big bunch of flowers and branches.

23.

A cold night. A fresh, clear morning and a cloudless sky. Lyova said yesterday that some of the oaks had begun to open up, while some of the lime-trees were in full leaf.

28.

Lyova went to Moscow last night—Masha[63] is very ill.

30.

The heat is unbearable, and there is thunder all day and night.

May 13.

Lyova brought in some wild roses in full bloom.

May 14.

Lyova, Stepa, and Serezha have gone to Nikolskoye.

15.

We bathed and had coffee, and then gathered mushrooms in our birch-wood. Very hot day.

Night from 16 to 17.

They've come back from Nikolskoye. Weather cold and dismal.

18.

Hannah“ went to Tula to buy some toys for the children. We went to gather mushrooms, were caught in a drizzle, and got chilled. Lyova was greatly upset yesterday because they hadn't sent the proofs, and wrote to Moscow telling Ries to send back the manuscript. He wrote to Lieven and Sasha to-day. There are big pods on the acacia-trees. It is dry and cold and windy.

May 26.

The heat is terrible. Lyova and Ilya went to Tula by train. I went bathing with the children. The wild roses have lost all their petals. They sold the hay from the garden yesterday.

February 13, 1873.

Lyova has gone to Moscow, and I have been sitting here all day staring into empty space, with my head full of painful, worrying thoughts. In this state of mental stress I invariably take to my diary ; I pour out my bad mood, and it helps to sober me up. My mood is stupid and wicked, painful and dishonest. For where would I be without him—him whom I love so deeply, and whose views on everything are so pure and noble? And yet in moments of anxiety I sometimes look into my own heart and ask myself what I really want. And much to my own horror, I reply : I want to have a good time, with flippant company, and new dresses, and I want to be admired and to hear people praise my beauty ; and I want Lyova to hear and see it all, and I should like to take him away for a little from his strenuous labours and make him spend some time with me, living the life of so many ordinary people. I indignantly refuse all things with which the devil tempts me, as he once tempted Eve, and yet it all makes me despise myself more than before. I hate the people who tell me I am beautiful; I have never believed it, and now it is too late. What good would this love have done me, anyway? My dear little Petya loves his old nurse as much as he could ever love the greatest beauty. Lyova could get used to the ugliest wife, so long as she was gentle and obedient and conformed to his mode of life. I am trying to turn myself inside out and discover everything which is false and mean and rotten within me. I am having my hair waved to-day, and I enjoy the thought that nobody will be there to see me and that it's really quite unnecessary. I like my new ribbons, and I also want a new leather belt, and now that I've written it all down I want to cry. . . .

The children upstairs are waiting for their music lesson, and, instead of that, I am sitting in the study, writing all this nonsense. We were out skating to-day; the boys had a row with Feodor Feodorovich; I felt sorry for them, and did my best to put F. F. in a good temper and at the same time to console the children. I don't particularly like the new English governess, who arrived two days ago; *elle est trop commune* and dreary. But it's difficult to say, yet.

April 17, 1873.

It snowed all morning, and, though it is five degrees above zero, there is still no grass, no warmth, no sunshine, and none of that sweet and melancholy feeling of spring, to which one looks forward so eagerly. My mind is as gloomy and cold and sad as the weather. Lyova is writing his novel, and it's going along well."

November 11, 1873.

At nine o'clock on the morning of November 9 my little Petya died of throat trouble. He died peacefully after only two days' illness. I nursed him for fourteen and a half months. He was born on the 13th of June, 1872. He was such a bright, happy child. My darling, I loved him so much, and now everything seems so empty since they buried him yesterday. My mind refuses to take in that my Petya and the dead baby are one and the same ; and yet I loved them both ; but what a difference ! The one such a bright, lively and affectionate little creature, the other so quiet and solemn, so cold and dead. He loved me very much ; I wonder if he was sorry to have to leave me here ?

February 17, 1874.

However much I may think about the future, I know that there is none. As soon as the grass begins to grow on Petya's little grave, they will have to dig it up for me ; the thought haunts me unceasingly.

October 12, 1875.

This everlasting country life is becoming unbearable. This dull, monotonous apathy day after day, year after year, is terrible. I wake up in the morning but don't get up. Why should I ? I know the cook will come along, and then the nurse to tell me that the servants are grumbling about the food, and that there is no sugar in the house and that it must be sent for ; and later on I'll sit down and, with a pain in my shoulder, start embroidering ; and after that, grammar lessons or scales on the piano, and, though I like doing it, I feel that I am not doing it as well as I should. And in the evening—the same sewing and embroidery, and Lyova and Auntie with their unbearable games of patience. I find some pleasure in reading—but how many good books are there ? Sometimes I feel that I only live in my dreams. I dream that I go to midnight Mass and that I pray as I never do when I am awake, or else I dream of marvellous picture galleries or of wonderful flowers, or of crowds of people whom, instead of hating and avoiding, I love with all my heart.

God knows that for a whole year I have struggled with all my might against this shameful feeling of boredom. I have been trying to persuade myself that it was best for the children, both physically and morally, to live in the country, and I succeeded, up to a point, in suppressing my own selfish feelings ; but now I see, much to my horror, that this life is bringing about a terrible state of apathy and a stupid animal-like indifference to everything, so that it terrifies me, and I am finding it even harder than before to struggle against my feeling of boredom.

Besides, I am not alone ; as the years go by, my life is becoming more and more closely linked up with Lyova's, and I can feel him drawing me into his own dismal, apathetic condition. It hurts me to see him in his present state. Dull and depressed, he spends weeks on end without any work, without joy or energy, just as though this condition satisfied him. I hate to see him die, mentally, and surely he can't go on like this for very long. Maybe my judgment is commonplace and entirely wrong. But I do believe that this atmosphere, which he has created, and which I find so oppressive, —this atmosphere of solitude and monotony—only tends to increase both his apathy and mine. And when I come to think of the future, when the children are grown up, of their life and desires and education, I begin to realise that Lyova is too indifferent and apathetic to be my helpmate, and that the whole moral responsibility for the children's failures and sufferings will ultimately rest on me ; yet how can I bring up the children *alone*, especially when I am always conscious that Lyova is in such a cold and hopeless state of inertia.

If one did not hope, life would be quite impossible ; and I still hope that God will once again light that flame in Lyova's mind which has kept him alive in the past, and which he will need for the future.

September 15, 1876.

A day of loneliness ; and here I am once again talking to my silent companion. In future, I mean to keep this diary daily, and conscientiously. Lyova went to Samara, and has now gone on from there to Orenburg, a town he always wanted to see. He sent me a wire from there. I am missing him very much and am feeling anxious. I am trying to persuade myself that I am glad that Lyova should be enjoying himself, but I am not : it hurts me to think that he could depart so cheerfully in the middle of this happy period of love and fellowship, and did not even seem to mind giving me this long and painful fortnight of sadness and anxiety.

I am determined to do my very best to put all my energy into the children's lessons, but I am so terribly impatient ! I lose my temper and shout at them, and to-day I was so annoyed with Serezha's essay on the Volga and his bad spelling, and with Ilya's laziness, that I burst into tears at the end of the lesson. The children were greatly surprised, and Serezha at once felt sorry for me, which touched me deeply. Afterwards he kept walking around me, and was so gentle and considerate. I am not too friendly with Tanya. It is sad to think of the constant war one has to wage with one's own children. I have no evil thoughts ; I only want more ease and freedom. I get terribly tired ; I am not feeling well, I am breathing heavily, and my indigestion gives me pain. I am all shrivelled up with the cold.

September 17.

My name-day. Another day has passed without Lyova or news from him. I got up this morning feeling lazy and unwell and bothered with all the daily worries. The children went out with Stepa to fly a kite, and came running in, lively and excited, to call me out. I didn't go. I got them to bring me Lyova's papers from the gun cupboard, and soon became absorbed in his manuscripts and diaries. A whole mass of new impressions passed through my mind, only I can't write down the biography which I thought out ; I shall never be able to be sufficiently impartial. I keep looking for certain pages in his diaries dealing with some former love-affair, and I grow so jealous that everything becomes dim and confused in my mind. But I shall try it all the same. I am afraid of my spiteful feelings because he went away, for I loved him so much during the last days he was here, and I can't help blaming him for having caused me so much sorrow and anxiety. He was so anxious about my health ; and yet he didn't seem to mind torturing me by going away at a time when it was particularly bad : it is hard to understand him. I can't sleep with all this anxiety, I hardly eat anything, and merely keep swallowing my tears, and weeping several times a day when I am alone. I am feverish and I shiver at night, and my head seems to be bursting with nervous excitement. How many different thoughts have passed through my mind during this fortnight ! I am getting on well with the children, but I seem to abuse my desire to make them feel sorry for me. It's such a joy to see them care so much. Tanya is getting very pretty ; her childish infatuation for Ippolit Nagornyi,·· the violinist, rather perturbs me. I didn't give them any lessons after lunch ; my energy seemed to have gone, and I was incapable of doing anything. Good God, help me to bear up for a few days more ! " Why is he punishing me ? " I keep thinking. " Is it because I love him so much ? " My happiness has suffered again, and it annoys me to think that my spontaneous outbreak of love and my short-lived happiness should have been nipped in the bud.

September 18, 1876.

I got a wire from Syzran to-day. He will arrive in the morning the day after to-morrow. I cheered up at once, and the lessons went far better ; everything seems so bright and happy in the house, and the children are lovely. But I have a pain in my chest ; I wonder if I'll be ill ; I was worried lest it should upset our peaceful, well-ordered life. It was very painful and tiring to speak so much during the lessons. The children came upstairs in a bad temper after M. Rey's lesson" ; they kept playing about all the time, and he gave them a *two* for behaviour. I told Serezha I would not let him go out shooting if he didn't learn how to behave himself, and hoped it would be a lesson to him ; but he suddenly flared up, saying, "*Au contraire*," and this hurt me very much. As he was saying good night, he asked me if I was still angry ; and I was so glad that I forgave him. Stepa is very sweet and is a great help to me in teaching the children and making them go over their lessons. When I think of Lyova coming the day after to-morrow, my heart leaps with joy, as though he were going to light the whole house with his presence.

February 27, 1877.

As I was reading over Lyova's diaries to-day, I came to the conclusion that I will not be able to write the "materials for his biography," as I originally intended. His mental life is so complicated, and his diaries excite me so much, that my thoughts grow confused and I stop seeing things clearly and reasonably. It's a pity to give up the idea. But what I can do is to record our present life and all the facts and conversations relating to his literary work ; I think I could do this conscientiously and with much interest. He has gone to Moscow to correct the proofs of the February number, and to see Zakharyin about his headaches and blood-pressure.

The other day, when I asked him to tell me something about his past, he said : " Please don't ask me such things ; it makes me too excited, and I am too old to live my life all over again by recalling it to memory."

September 21, 1878.

Nicholas Tolstoy[68] was here. We discussed the proposed plan of going to Moscow with him and his young wife.

September 22.

Lyova and Ilya went shooting with the hounds, and brought back six hares. Andryusha was vaccinated to-day.

September 23.

Our wedding anniversary : sixteen years. I taught the children German ; they did very well. A warm, lovely day. Andryusha gives me great joy.

September 27, 1878.

Sunday. I got up late. Lyova went to Mass ; the three of us had coffee together—Lyova, Mashenka (his sister), and myself. After lunch the children walked to Yasenki. Mashenka and Ulyaninsky[69] (Serezha's Greek and Latin tutor) went to Tula. Lyova and Serezha went shooting with the hounds, and I stayed at home to cut out jackets for the boys. Then Masha, Annie,[70] and I drove to Yasenki ; to join the children. Just before we left, Prince Urusov arrived with his gun, and went off to look for our huntsmen. In Yasenki we discovered the children in a shop, buying and eating sweets. Everybody turned up for dinner. In the twilight, after dinner, Lyova, Ilya, and I played a game of croquet against M. Nief,[71] little Lyova, and Urusov[72]; they won. In the evening Lyova and Urusov played chess ; the children kept eating sweets and were in a boisterous mood ; I read Octave Feuillet's *Journal d'une femme*. Very fine and noble, only the end is unnatural. The whole thing seems to have been written as a protest against the new, and all too realistic, modern literature. It is midnight now. Lyova is having supper, and then we are going to bed.

September 25, 1878.

I taught the children in the morning. Mashenka came for dinner, bringing Anton, Rossa, and Nadya Delvig[73] with her. The children were delighted. After dinner they danced a quadrille, and, to make up the set, little Lyova and I took part in it too ; Lyova and Alexander Grigoryevich[74] played the piano ; later on Mashenka played the piano and Alexander Grigoryevich the violin, and it went rather well. They played Mozart's delightful sonata the *andante* of which always brings tears to my eyes. After that Lyova played Weber's sonatas. But this time Alexander Grigoryevich's fiddle made a rather poor show, as compared with Nagornyi's playing. At the end they played Beethoven's "Kreutzer Sonata" ; it went badly ; but what a wonderful piece it *must* be when it's properly played ! Afterwards the children and I played a game of *fate** with the guests. Rossa is very charming and

* A card game.

pleasant, but rather ungainly to look at. They all spent the night here.

The next day, 26.

I woke up with a headache. Lyova and Anton went to Mass. The rest of the company had a very gay time playing croquet. The weather is lovely ; the leaves are all yellow, but haven't fallen yet, and everything is so beautiful. The nights are frosty, and there is a full moon. After lunch Rossa and I played another game of croquet against Anton and Serezha. Lyova persuaded the children to go for a cross-country walk with the dogs.

Each one took a hound on the leash, including a huntsman on horseback ; Annie, Mlle. Gachet, and M. Nief went too. It made such a fine picture. After croquet, when they had gone, I went to see Vasili Ivanovich, and felt very sad and embarrassed. On his return, Serezha went there too, and was surprised to see me. He likes Vasili Ivanovich[76] and never forgets him ; I'm very glad he doesn't.

Lyova also went shooting, and killed a partridge in the new birch-wood. The children played croquet until dinner-time, while I watched them. The Delvigs went off after dinner, and the children all crowded in Lyova's drawing-room, talking and laughing and playing games. They went early to bed.

September 27.

A clear, dry day. I was busy cutting out and sewing, and teaching Lisa French, and Masha and Tanya German. I am in a tidy, matter-of-fact frame of mind. Andryusha was vaccinated on Friday, and he is restless and unwell ; my nipples are hurting me. Lyova went out shooting with the hounds to the Zaseka wood, but didn't even see anything ; his work is at a standstill, and he has a pain in his back. Mashenka seems discontented, and feels cold and unhappy.

Sunday, October 1.

Lyova drove to church in the morning. Ulyaninsky gave Serezha his Greek and Latin lesson. I stayed in bed late, as I hadn't slept because of Andryusha's vaccination, which keeps troubling him at night. All the children dressed up in their Sunday best and waited anxiously for me, because they wanted to go to the Delvigs, and the weather was getting bad. But, as it was quite warm, I let them go. The whole four of them drove away, along with Mlle. Gachet. Urusov arrived, and went with Lyova and M. Nief to shoot snipe. Mashenka is ill, and was busy trying her homœopathic cure, and I was left quite alone. After a stroll round the house and the croquet lawn I came back and sat down to sew. We had dinner at seven, and then sat around, talking pleasantly on serious subjects. Lyova and Urusov had a game of chess, while I embroidered Andryusha's dress. The children came back after nine o'clock, very pleased with their day and eager to tell us all about it.

October 2.

We were in the middle of our lesson when someone drove up to the house. It turned out to be Gromov and his daughter, Nadya, who is engaged to Nicholas

[Tolstoy]. She is a very attractive and serious-minded girl, very natural in her ways. I am sure I shall like her very much. They went away immediately after dinner, and I worked all evening, and later on had a bath with Tanya. Everything is peaceful and happy, and by no means dull. The weather is fine, and we are having lovely moonlight nights. Andryusha is better.

October 3.

In spite of the lovely weather, I have stayed indoors all day. I tutored the children, and scolded and punished Tanya for not going out for a walk, and for running away from Mlle. Gachet. Mashenka kept me company and was in a very good mood. Lyova went out hunting and brought back five hares ; his horse fell and he fell with it, but, thank God, only hurt his arm, though he turned a complete somersault over the horse's head ; the horse twisted its neck, and was unable to get up for quite a while. Serezha applied a Spanish fly to his right side ; I am still a little worried about him. Andryusha is a perfect darling ; he picks up his bread himself and drinks his milk like a good boy. Nicholas is coming to-morrow. The children played croquet after their lessons. While Lyova was dining after coming back from hunting, a letter suddenly arrived from my sister Tanya ; I was so overjoyed that I read it aloud to everybody present. When I got to the part where she sent her regards to " our kind, gentle, holy, and buxom *papa* " (we had got all these epithets from the popular *Oracle* book, and always referred to Lyova as *our papa* at croquet), all the children burst out laughing.

October 4, 1878.

It is Tanya's fourteenth birthday. After getting up, I took the children to the wood, where a picnic had been prepared for them. M. Nief was then in his shirt-sleeves busy making *une omelette* and hot chocolate, and there were four smouldering bonfires, over which Serezha was roasting a *shashlyk*. Everything went off splendidly, and the children ate a lot, and, above all, the weather was perfect. We played croquet when we came back, and, all of a sudden, noticed our Samara horses and donkeys coming along the avenue. The children were so excited, and at once ran away and jumped on the donkeys' backs. Nicholas came to dinner, with Baroness Delvig and Rossa. We drank Tanya's health in champagne, and she blushed, but was very pleased all the same. In the evening Tanya and I drove the visitors back to Kozlovka, and went to bed late. We met Lyova on our way back ; he had come out to meet us.

October 6.

I am ill ; I have a gumboil and my back is so sore. I went to see Lyova in the morning. He was sitting at the table downstairs, busy writing. He told me that he was starting his new book for the tenth time. It is to begin with a cross-examination of a case between a number of peasants and a landowner. He got this idea of the case from some genuine documents, and is even going to leave in the actual date. This case is going to be like a fountain, scattering events into the peasant world, into the landowner's home, to Petersburg, and other places where certain characters will play a part.

I like this *entrée en matière* very much.[76] The children are rather lazy about their work, and are trying to distract themselves with other matters.

October 8.

Nicholas has got married. Lyova went to Tula, where he acted as "wedding father," and Tanya and I drove straight to the church. The ceremony had almost started by the time we arrived. We drove back again when it was finished. Serezha was out hunting, and got two hares. This morning the children went to Yasenki on their donkeys.

October 9.

Bibikov[77] arrived with bad news from Samara ; the estate has again brought in hardly anything at all. I grew terribly angry, for I hadn't been told before that the land had been leased, and that some cattle had been bought, and that the harvest was poor. I had a terrible quarrel with Lyova. I am feeling intensely miserable, although I don't feel at all guilty ; but how I hate it all !—myself, and my life, and my so-called *happiness* ! It bores and disgusts me. . . .

October 11.

D. A. Dyakov came in the morning. He had been driving about looking for an estate for his daughter. Lyova was out hunting, but didn't kill anything. Yesterday he shot two snipe, and the dogs caught a hare for him. In the evenings we read aloud. M. Nief reads Alexandre Dumas's *Trois Mousquetaires*, which is very entertaining. The children are greatly interested in it, and wait impatiently for the evening. Lyova is busy reading up material for his new book, but keeps complaining that his head is tired, and says he is weary and can't write. We are very friendly again, and I have decided to spare him all worry.

October 13.

I was busy studying with Lyova and Lisa, when suddenly the other children, shrieking with joy, came running in to tell us that Sergei Nikolaevich had come back from Tula, where he had gone on business. We spent the whole day talking.

October 14.

Mashenka left us to-day. Sergei Nikolaevich went to Yasenki to see Khomyakov and to get some information about a factor for the estate. Lyova went out shooting and got six partridges. Sergei Nikolaevich asked several times about my sister Tanya ; he hasn't forgotten her, and said he was very anxious to speak to her the day he met her at the station. Serezha hit little Lyova, who in his turn threw a stick at him. Before that Serezha had wanted to take the stick away from him. I was very angry with Serezha, and gave him a severe scolding. The drawing-master (the hunchback) came in the evening. He is teaching Tanya, Ilya, and little Lyova. Tanya takes the work seriously, but the boys keep laughing and playing about. Ulyaninsky gave Serezha his Latin and Greek lesson, and afterwards we again listened to *Les Trois Mousquetaires*, which the children continue to enjoy. I'm in a strange mood. I am much taken up with my appearance, and have been dreaming of a life quite different from ours. I should like to read a lot and become more educated, and take part in discussions, and be beautiful ; I keep thinking of dresses and other silly things like that. I am thinking of taking the children to Moscow. I am terribly fond of Andryusha.

Sunday, October 15.

When I came down for tea this morning, I found Lyova in the drawing-room, with his brother Sergei, the children, and the two masters—the hunchback and Ulyaninsky, the tutor. The presence of the teachers is a little embarrassing. Lyova drove to church. Preparations were made to hunt. Seven horses were saddled, and Lyova rode off with the hounds, and with his brother Serezha, little Serezha, Ilya, M. Nief, and two servants. Tanya, Masha, little Lyova, Mlle. Gachet, and Lisa went on donkeys to Kozlovka. I stayed alone in the house, looking after Andryusha, but, when he fell asleep, I had nothing else to do, and so I had them get the cart ready for me, and drove off to meet the children. I met them at the boundary of the estate, and, taking Mlle. Gachet with me, drove home again, where I ordered some *kvass* and grated horseradish, which we had, and then didn't have dinner till the others returned. The huntsmen came back after six, looking cheerful and contented. They brought back six hares, strung up on a stick, which they brought into the room, with great pomp. In the evening we had more Dumas ; the children were very tired ; Serezha was very pleasant, saying a lot of nice things about the children. I am going to bed.

October 16.

I got up late this morning and, as usual, the children came into my room one by one ; and afterwards Lyova came. Andryusha, who was sleeping in my room—for I had just been nursing him—was taken away ; I then tried on my new dress, which is very fine. Then I had a talk with Serezha, the brother, who was in very low spirits, and then we all saw him off to Pirogovo. I made little Lyova and Ilya read German. After dinner, Lyova went to Tula to attend a high school meeting, as he is the procurator. I have undertaken to write a short life of Lyova[78] for a volume of the new *Russian Library*, consisting of extracts from his works chosen by Strakhov. It is to be published by Stasulevich. I discovered that it was by no means easy to write a biography. I wrote a little of it, but even that was no good. The children were in my way, and the nursing and the noise around me. Besides, I didn't know enough of Lyova's life before our marriage. I tried to use Pushkin's, Lermontov's, and Gogol's biographies as models, and became absorbed in reading their poetry, which I love so much. It's a pity that even poets should have so many faults ; Lermontov's biography spoils him greatly in my eyes. I read a little more Dumas ; the children are more and more interested in him each day. I also sewed a flannel vest for Andryusha. I am now reading *L'idée de Jean Têterol*, by Cherbulliez ; I like it very much. As Lyova is away, Mlle. Gachet is keeping me company. Lyova wasn't working to-day, but this morning he said: "It's going to be excellent."

October 18, 1878.

Andryusha was unwell; he was feverish, and his stomach was out of order. I got up late. The children have gone out; the boys have gone with the dogs into the fields to catch mice, while the girls and little Lyova have gone donkey-riding. Lyova has gone out hunting. I played croquet with Mlle. Gachet and Vasili Ivanovich. We won one game and Mlle. Gachet the other. It is warm and clear outside, and there is a south wind blowing. I have taken up music again with little Lyova. The dinner was very bad; the potato soup smelt of lard, the pie was too dry, the *livanshiks* were like shoe-leather, and I don't eat hare. I only had some *vinaigrette*, and after dinner I gave the cook a row. By that time Lyova came back with four hares and a fox; he was silent and meditative. He keeps reading a great deal. To-day the post brought a piece of silk that Tanya had sent from the Caucasus, and Schuyler's English translation of *The Cossacks*,[19] which is rather well done. In the evening we had more Dumas, while I was busy cutting a white cashmere frock for Andryusha, which I want to embroider in red silk. Ilya and little Lyova were being bathed downstairs; they laughed and played about. I went to have a look at them after they were put to bed; they looked so lovely and clean and happy. I went in on the pretext of seeing about Ilya's night-shirt, which he had said was too short for him. I feel mentally dull, and feel the need for some new impressions and *émotions*.

October 21.

Andryusha was very ill yesterday; his little hands and feet got quite cold, and he developed a high temperature; he cried and shivered in his sleep, and his mouth and eyes kept twitching. To-day the fever went down, but he has now got diarrhœa. His sleep is very restless, and it worries me a great deal. Navrotsky, the editor of a new magazine, the *Russkaya Rech*, has come from Petersburg. He read us some poems and some fragments of a play—not bad. He told us a lot of Petersburg news, and was quite interesting. The teachers have come again: this is Saturday. We had pancakes to-day. I had a serious talk with Serezha; I had told him yesterday that I didn't like him to tease all the others, and now I told him that, if I reproached him, I always did it lovingly, for I wanted my children to be happy, since happiness consisted chiefly of being loved by everyone. I've been thinking that it is a pity that monarchs should be embalmed—"*dust ye are, and to dust ye shall return*"—and all this embalming and these mausoleums are really a curse. Lyova was out hunting, and took one hare. He wrote something yesterday, but hasn't shown it to me. The weather is poor; there is a fine drizzle outside. Serezha has been having a pain in his side for the last three days.

Sunday, 22.

The children walked or rode on their donkeys to Yasenki, and Masha went with them in the carriage, drawn by Kolpik. They got some sweets there and ate them. Annie and I stayed with Andryusha, who isn't really well yet. I was cutting out a bib for him, and altogether had a very dull day. In the morning the hunchback teacher told us the very interesting story of how he had started his career as a draughtsman, in a silk factory. Lyova was out at Mass, after which he and Serezha went out hunting. But they had no luck. Nurse has gone to Tula, and I have been with Andryusha ever since seven this morning, and am very tired. Lyova wanted to write some letters, but only wrote two, one to Turgenev, the other to Strakhov, and after that stopped. In the evening the children played hide-and-seek and other games and I read Cherbulliez's *L'idée de Jean Têterol*. It's rather good. Lyova was reading, and then fell asleep.

October 23, 1878.

After having coffee with me, Lyova went out hunting to the Zaseka wood. I taught Masha Russian, Lisa French, and little Lyova German. Lyova came back for dinner, bringing three hares with him. Serezha played Haydn's violin sonata quite well, Alexander Grigoryevich played the violin part. In the evening Lyova played Weber's and Schubert's sonatas, also accompanied on the violin, while I embroidered Andryusha's white cashmere dress in red silk, listening to the music with much pleasure. It is windy and unpleasant outside. Lyova said to-day that he had read so much historical material that he would like a rest and read Dickens's *Martin Chuzzlewit* for a change. I know that when Lyova begins to read English novels he is sure to start writing again himself. The children are flourishing. Little Lyova is well with his lessons ; Ilya is busy with her embroidery ; and Masha has such a meek little expression, which, however, I quite fail to fathom. Tanya is brooding and lazy, with neither energy nor whims. (A man has destroyed all the mice and rats in the house, and was paid 5 roubles for it.)

October 24.

It was raining when we got up but later on it cleared up. We watched while they lowered Mishka with a rope into the well to get out the pails. He managed to get out the two old pails, but could not find the new one. We spent some time in the store-room, going over the summer clothes that were being put away for the winter. I coached the children, and then went on with my sewing. I carried Andryusha about the house, and noticed how he shrieked with joy at the sight of the pictures and paintings on the walls. After dinner I had a lively time with the children, when we discussed the possibility of acting a play after Christmas. We are still reading extracts from *Les Trois Mousquetaires*. Lyova went hunting to Zakaz, but brought back nothing. He is dull and irritable, but we are happy and on the best of terms. He is still unable to write. To-day he said : " If ever I write anything again, I shall write in such a way that the children can read every word of it."

October 25.

I gave little Lyova his music-lesson, and searched for an easy *menuet* among Haydn's Symphonies. Then I worked at a white piqué dress for Andryusha. Lyova was out hunting, and brought back a hare and another little animal very like a weasel. In the evening we discussed the outline of Lyova's biography. He talked, and I wrote down what he said. We got along very well, and I am so glad we did it. The children are working hard. Wind and pelting rain outside. We read more Dumas in the evening.

October 27.

This morning I sent Lyova's ten letters to the post, and went down for my usual solitary tea. I sat there, all alone, in a state of depression, gulping back my tears ; then, as it was a fine morning, I went out for a stroll. Lyova had gone off hunting early in the morning. I played with Andryusha for a while, and then went out for a walk to look for the children. I found the three boys among the haystacks, with M. Nief lying among the hay, reading a book. I didn't see the girls, though. It was lovely in the garden. I was angry with Ilya and little Lyova, before dinner, for stealing some caviar ; I smacked Ilya and gave them both a good scolding. In the evening I took all the children and the governors for a drive in the moonlight ; it was a glorious night. Then I wrote Lyova's biographical sketch. Andryusha was feverish yesterday ; and Alexey Alexeyevich Bibikov came to see us. I'm going to supper now to have some boiled spike, and after supper I'll nurse the child and then go to bed.

October 28.

I had tea all by myself, then Tanya came along and said she had a sore throat. I looked at it, and found a little slimy swelling on one side. I was much upset, and sent her to gargle with Bertholet salts—one teaspoon to a tumbler of hot water. But, as she is quite well otherwise, I've stopped worrying. I went to the wood to see how the barrels were getting on ; we have undertaken to make 6,000 barrels for Gill.[80] I went by the path through the wood ; it was such a beautiful, clear, frosty day. Afterwards I went for a walk with Masha, Annie, and Mlle. Gachet, and the boys once again played about on the haystacks. Their tutors came after dinner. Tanya drew a woman's head quite well in charcoal. I worked at a christening robe for Parasha's baby, and bathed Andryusha for the first time since his vaccination. Lyova was out hunting, but only brought back one hare.

October 29.

The house is in a terrible state. The poisoned rats had died under the floors, and the odour was so dreadful that all the floors had to be torn up. It had been snowing, but later it got warm and muddy. The children played hide-and-seek and were very noisy, but, at any rate, they enjoyed themselves. I stayed in all day because of the weather. Lyova tried to settle down to work, and I finished his biographical sketch ; it took me the whole day. We had some reading at night, and I finished the christening robe.

Wednesday, November 1, 1878.

This morning Lyova read to me the beginning of his new book.[81] It is going to be a long, interesting, and ambitious work. It starts with a dispute between the peasants and the landowner over a plot of land, the arrival in Moscow of Prince Chernyshev and his family, the laying of the foundation-stone of the Church of the Saviour, an old woman pilgrim, etc. Dyakov came for dinner. Lyova killed a hare. In the evening we talked about the estates which Dyakov had been inspecting for Masha. On Monday Serezha and Tanya christened Parasha's baby ; they behaved very well, although Ilyusha and little Lyova giggled all the time. I went to Tula to-day with Dmitri Alexeyevich, Serezha, and Tanya ; it was a bright, frosty morning. We bought material for Tanya's winter coat, a furlined jacket for Serezha (12 silver roubles), and ordered a winter overcoat for him (65 silver roubles), shoes for Tanya, a jacket for me, lined with our own fox fur, as well as many other things. Lyova was working at home, but came to meet us on our return. It is always such a joy on going home to see his grey overcoat in the distance. Andryusha is well and bright. We brought the boys some tops at 10 copeks each, a thimble for Masha, beads and brooches and ear-rings for the dolls, and warm gloves for everybody. I was terribly tired, for we hadn't eaten anything all day, except some cakes and a bit of currant bread. In the evening I washed Andryusha. He has still got no hair on the top of his head, which rather worries me. We finished the *Trois Mousquetaires* with much interest. Lyova spent much of the evening improvising at the piano—he seems to have a special gift for it. I got a letter from Tanya ; Miss McCarthy has left her, and he wants to take Annie in her place ; but I can't let her go yet. I don't know what to do.

November 4.

I didn't write anything yesterday; I was too worried. Lyova and Serezha went out hunting, and there was such a mist that they lost their way and did not come back till nine at night. They just missed three foxes, and only brought back a hare. I went out to-day to see Lyova off to the hunt. The girls had a ride on their donkeys. The tutors came; we read aloud a little of a book which we all found very dull. Lyova isn't doing any writing at all, and is feeling much discouraged. I worked on a pair of flannel knickers for Tanya and embroidered Andryusha's handkerchiefs. I coached the children, and had an argument with Lyova about Serezha's French lessons. I maintained that he ought to be taught French literature, but Lyova didn't agree. Andryusha's nurse pierced holes in Masha's ears for her ear-rings.

November 5.

A lonely Sunday, and such a lonely, dull, foggy day. Lyova and Serezha went out hunting, and Serezha brought back a hare. The other children, with Annie, Mlle. Gachet, and M. Nief went to Yasenki with their donkeys and a cart, and bought a lot of sweets. I worked a lot, and spent much time on Andryusha. His bald spot and the unusual size of his head rather puzzle me. At night they played Mozart's Trio as a duet; Lyova had his supper, and read the whole time, as he always does at supper and breakfast. I had tea and some sauerkraut. I finished reading "Les deux Barbeux" in the *Revue des Deux Mondes*, and found it quite interesting. Tanya, Ilya, and little Lyova had their drawing-lesson this morning, and Serezha studied Greek and Latin with Ulyaninsky. Tanya has become quite good at shading. I must have taught her the elements of the thing quite well ; I taught her for three years, and it is only her fourth lesson with her new teacher.

November 6.

A foggy, depressing day. I read German with little Lyova, and, later, with Ilya. I taught Masha Russian and she really recited Pushkin's " Snowstorm " quite well ; but her writing was so bad, that I tore a sheet out of her copy-book. Alexander Grigoryevich was here ; he doesn't teach Ilya and little Lyova properly.

Lyova went out shooting, and brought back two hares. It worries him not to be able to write ; in the evening he was reading Dickens's *Dombey and Son*, and suddenly said to me : " I've got an idea ! " I asked him what it was, and though at first he didn't want to tell me, he finally said : " I have been thinking of an old woman, imagining her figure, her appearance, and her thoughts ; but I couldn't find a *feeling* to put into her, and now I've got it : it's the constant, everlasting feeling that Gerasimovich, her old man, locked up in jail and with his head shaven, is innocent." Then he sat down at the piano and improvised. I read the articles on art in the *Revue des Deux Mondes*. I've been knitting a blanket for Andryusha. At night the children talked about affectation, and accused Tanya of having behaved unnaturally during their recent visit to the Delvigs. Everybody is very well.

November 7.

I cut out shirts for Lyova, coached Lisa, and had rather an unpleasant bother : I thought someone had cut a bit of linen from the length, and began to accuse certain people ; but afterwards I measured it again, and found that there wasn't any missing. Lyova took Ilya and little Lyova to the bath-house at night ; he is in a much better frame of mind now that he is getting his ideas straight. I am still worried about Andryusha's head. Tanya has a slightly sore throat ; I examined her on the history of Alexander Nevski to-day ; she didn't know it very well. I told little Lyova about Moses and the ten plagues of Egypt.

November 10, 1878.

I haven't written anything for three days. I had a headache, and Andryusha wasn't well, with a dry cough and a cold ; but he is better now. Lyova, too, has been indoors all day, which is unusual ; but he, too, has a cold and a slight temperature. I tutored little Lyova, made him translate from English, and told him about the exodus of the Jews from Egypt, and then we practised Haydn's *menuet* for four hands. Masha wrote an essay, a description of her room, learned Zhukovsky's " Svetlana " off by heart, and read aloud. Her father gave her her first lesson in arithmetic ; it took her all her time to understand what 20, 50, 60, etc., meant. We grumbled at Tanya to-day ; she is so very lazy. I played some duets with Lyova in the evening, and worked at an apron of unbleached linen for Masha and read *Le Roman d'un*

Peintre, which I found rather dull. We have just had tea and some salt fish ; to-day, being Friday, Lyova won't eat any meat. I have arranged for Akulka, Nurse's granddaughter, to be taken into the orphanage, and Uncle Sergei is taking her to Tula to-morrow. We are getting the skates ready, for the sky is grey with big clouds sailing across it ; it is cold and feels like snow—it's about time it started ! I'm feeling like a machine, and should like to have a little life to myself, but it's no good . . . no more of that . . . not a word . . . silence !

November 11.

It's a pity I always have to write my diary at night, when I'm tired. Last night Andryusha suddenly began to choke and cough ; went on from four till eight in the morning. I got a terrible fright. But then it grew better, though he still has a sharp, hoarse cough, and diarrhœa. I gave him three drops of antimony, and soaked a piece of flannel in some oil, camphor, soap, and lard, and put it round his throat. Lyova said to-day that everything had become clear in his mind, and that all the characters were taking shape ; he works quite cheerfully now, with *faith* in his task. But he keeps coughing and has a headache. The drawing-master and Ulyaninsky came to-day. Tanya drew a shepherd's head quite well, but Ilya and Lyova are drawing merely to amuse themselves. I did quite a lot of work, and finished a flannel vest for Andryusha, as well as a pillow and two pillow-slips, which were also for him. Got a letter from Mother.

November 14.

Serezha, Tanya, Ilya, little Lyova, and I went to Tula on Sunday. It was dark and muddy, but quite warm. The children enjoyed themselves very much ; we got to the Delvig's by six ; Serezha was already there, he had gone there with his tutor earlier in the day. The children danced and played games, and it was a joy to watch them. Obolensky came to see us on Sunday morning ; Lyova spent the evening at home, but came to meet us when we got back at night. He had a headache. The Delvigs gave me some of Sollogub's *vaudevilles*, so that I could choose one for the children's party after Christmas. We read one of them yesterday ; it's called *A Russian Painter's Studio* ; I think it'll do. Anyway, most of the fun is in the rehearsals and preparations. Last night Lyova and Alexander Grigoryevich played a violin-and-piano duet. This morning, after a bad night, full of dreams and nightmares, I had tea with Lyova ; it happens so seldom ; and we had a long philosophic discussion on the meaning of life and death, and on religion, etc. Such talks with Lyova always have a soothing effect on me. I find certain points in his wisdom which give me consolation and solve many of my difficulties. I should like to quote his views, but I can't do it now—I am so tired and my head aches.

Lyova goes out hunting every day. He brought back six hares yesterday and to-day he went out with his hounds and shot a fox. D. D. Obolensky[61] was here again ; his affairs are in a very bad state, and he seems to pour out all his sorrows when he comes here. Lyova is not very well, nor is Andryusha, with his diarrhœa, but he is quite cheerful in spite of it.

November 16.

Lyova said : " The ideas, the characters, and the plot are all complete in my head." But he is still unwell, and is not able to write. He began to eat lenten food yesterday ; I keep objecting to it, for I am sure that it is not good for him. He stayed at home to-day, but was out hunting yesterday, and brought back three hares and a fox.

I helped little Lyova with his Russian grammar ; later I examined Tanya on the reign of Ivan III, but she didn't know it at all. Masha read and copied. I got out my tapestry to embroider. Serezha and Tanya keep looking for *amusements*, and I am sorry I can give them so few but I'll do my best. We all gathered in the drawing-room at night—Lyova, I, and our six children—and it suddenly made me sad to think that some day we would all be scattered and would look back on that evening. I got a letter from Tanya to-day, and yesterday heard from Strakhov and Lisa Obolensky. I keep on asking Lyova to correct the biographical sketch I wrote, but he won't listen to me.

Sunday, November 19, 1878.

Yesterday Lyova hunted down four hares and a fox and to-day, after working in the morning, he went to Mass. Thank heaven, I've persuaded him to stop eating lenten food ; his stomach was beginning to give him a lot of trouble. He read over his biography and said that it wasn't bad but that he hadn't corrected it yet. Serezha, Ilya, and M. Nief rode to Yasenki to see the Emperor pass ; but they only saw the train and *le marmiton*, as M. Nief jokingly said. Much to their joy

Tanya and little Lyova went on horseback, while Masha and Mlle. Gachet went in the cart. Tanya kept watching gleefully the train of my black skirt, which she had put on. We had a great to-do with Ilya on Friday. He refused to work and was disobedient and rude to M. Nief, and kept throwing a wet sponge at him, so that Lyova decided to make him go without dinner. When I went down to the children's room, I found him lying on his bed, sobbing bitterly, with his head hanging over the edge. I felt very sorry for him, and M. Nief and I did our best to console him, though he didn't get his dinner all the same. But what an appetite the poor boy had for his roast beef at supper !

In the evening we had quadrilles ; the children danced so wholeheartedly : first the older ones, and then the little ones.

My sad autumn mood has come over me once again. I sew or read in silence, and feel dull and indifferent to everything, and all the future is dark. The drawing-room window is still open ; it is foggy but quite warm outside.

Tuesday, November 21.

A lot of petty annoyances : Nurse is pregnant and will have to go away in two months. I'll have to get poor Andryusha a new one. Grigori[82] gave me notice. Lyova and Ilya were out hunting, and brought back six hares. Serezha had a cough, and he and Tanya stayed in all day playing waltzes ; Serezha also played Beethoven's Sonata-Fantasia. In the evening they danced quadrilles and other dances. Andryusha has diarrhœa and is very weak. It is warm outside, and the children have brought in some catkins.

Friday, November 24, 1878.

I have been feverish for three days, with a cough and toothache. It is still warm and no sign of snow. Grigori has gone. Andryusha still has diarrhœa ; he is learning to walk on all fours now. Little Lyova was telling me to-day about the wanderings of the Jews in the desert, but suddenly he stopped, and, realising that the lesson had already lasted for an hour and that he would have to go over it again, he burst out sobbing : " I can't, I can't ! You can give me a *one.*" So we stopped then, and, fortunately, I was very patient and didn't lose my temper, but left the lesson over till to-morrow.

I am feeling very gloomy. Lately I have been having some jealous thoughts and suspicions about Lyova. I sometimes feel it is a kind of madness, and keep asking God for help. For I certainly should go mad if anything like that were to happen.

I still nurse Andryusha at night. It is silent, and only the ikon lamp flickers dimly in the dark. Nurse has gone to dry the baby's clothes* . . . I covered up Tanya and Masha, who had thrown off their clothes in their sleep and went to bed myself. I was feverish last night, and couldn't sleep. Tanya's fur coat, jacket, and cap have arrived. My fox-fur coat is too narrow at the back, and the sleeves are too short.

Lyova has been in these last two days ; he went to Tula on Wednesday and had dinner with the Samarins. I wrote another biographical sketch to-day, but it's too long, and so, once again, is no good.

* Twenty-nine words are missing in the Russian text, which is edited by Sergei Tolstoy (the young Serezha of the *Diary*), and a few sentences (marked here in each case) have apparently been left out for " family reasons."

December, 18, 1879.

Another year has gone past. I am anxiously waiting for my confinement, which is already overdue. The thought of another child depresses me ; my whole horizon seems to have been narrowed down. Everybody in the house is in a state of nervousness ; Christmas is near, and my confinement is still uncertain. It has been terribly cold—more than 20 below zero. Masha had a bad throat and a temperature for a week, but she got up to-day. Lyova has gone to Tula in order to send Bibikov to Moscow about the new edition, and has promised to buy something for the Christmas-tree. He writes a great deal on religious subjects. Andryusha brightens my whole life—he is a joy of a child.

Two days after this Misha was born. It happened at six o'clock in the morning on the 20th of December, in the year 1879.

February 11, 1880.

NOTES ON THE HEALTH OF MY LITTLE ONES

Andryusha is two years and two months old ; Misha seven and a half weeks. Andryusha got up at seven, drank acorn coffee and milk. He wet his bed once ; he put on a shirt open at the neck, a thin vest, knickers, stockings with garters at the side ; a flannel suit in the morning, and a white one through the day. He ate an egg at eleven, asked for a white rusk, and went to sleep. He speaks very little, but sometimes manages to pronounce some quite difficult words almost correctly. I feed Misha every two or three hours ; he is often constipated. I still bathe him daily, he keeps sucking a rubber teat dipped in sugar-water. He has begun to smile now in a conscious way.

At night I roll him in a quilt or a knitted shawl and a clean sheet, and fold a piece of flannel several times to serve as a napkin. I rinse out his mouth with water and wine at least twice a day.

Andryusha sleeps from twelve till two ; and at four has his dinner of soup, a cutlet, and some baked apple or *kissel.* At six he has some cold meat, and at eight some milk, and then is put to bed.

12, 1880.

Andryusha slept better last night, though he woke up a few times, and wet his bed twice ; this doesn't happen every night. He drank acorn coffee and milk in the morning, and had some cold turkey at eleven. He then slept from twelve till half-past one. When I got up, I washed the scrofulous sore on his knee with water and the soft soap I got at the chemist's, and then put on some glycerine. He has a slight cold in his head ; he played with his dolls, rocking them on his knee and giving them food, and then danced about. He had oatmeal broth for dinner and a little piece of roast beef, a raw Crimean apple, and stewed prunes and peaches. At night he drinks tea made of blackcurrant leaves and milk, and goes to bed at eight. He still has to be rocked and sung to sleep. His nights are rather restless ; he talks and moans in his sleep.

19, 1880.

Misha is well. I wrap him up at night, but during the day he wears a flannel vest, a bonnet, and a *bavette.*

I give him the breast every two and occasionally every three hours. It's the same at night. When he is restless, he gets a rubber teat dipped in sugar-water. At night he is rolled in his clothes and covered with a sheet and warm blanket. I bath him daily except Sunday, in thirty degrees Réaumur. He is often constipated, and sometimes have to give him warm enemas with almond-oil.

February 25.

Andryusha's stomach is out of order. Misha coughs a lot at night. Andryusha had a bath on Saturday and Wednesday—he thoroughly enjoys it. I haven't been giving Misha a bath for the last few days. Andryusha had some chicken-broth and a cutlet and a baked apple, but he hardly ate anything, and keeps asking for sweets, and often comes to see if he can find any on my bed-table, saying that those on the bed-table are *ours*, while the ones on the dressing-table are *papa's*. He plays with Vasya Matrenin, and dances to the tune of the concertina, and builds houses with plaids and blankets. He has a great passion for sponges, which he keeps kissing, sucking, or biting. He sometimes bites me, not spitefully, but merely out of exuberance. Misha laughed out aloud for the first time to-day when he was looking at a little bottle of eau-de-Cologne. When he isn't asleep, he wears a little bonnet, a flannel vest, and a *bavette*. He was taken out twice to-day in these clothes. For the past three days Andryusha has not wet either his bed or his drawers. He still has sores on his knee.

March 1.

Andryusha has a cough and still is having attacks of diarrhœa at least three times a day. He is pale and weak, and sleeps badly. Misha is constipated ; I gave him an enema to-day.

March 1, 1880.

My little boys are well. Yesterday I sent Matrena away, who had been looking after Misha, and kept only Nurse. I got Varya to take care of Andryusha. I have started giving Misha some ordinary milk mixed with a little water and sugar. I give him a small glassful through a rubber teat at four o'clock. He's been having it for five days now, and it has done away with his constipation, but has brought on diarrhœa.

March 15.

Andryusha has had a hoarse cough for the past two days ; he is weak and perspires a lot, although he is cheerful on the whole. He eats well.

March 27.

Misha eats milk porridge made with breadcrumbs —two spoonfuls in two-thirds of a cup of milk and one-third of water. In the morning he has milk through his rubber teat—two-thirds boiled milk and one-third water. His stomach has been out of order these last two days, but it's all right again now. At night he sometimes drinks a whole tumblerful of boiled milk, and also has some through the day before going to sleep. He has an egg and some meat or soup at eleven in the forenoon, and at dinner, at five o'clock, he has soup and meat, and sometimes some *kissel*. At eight he again eats a little meat, and has tea made of black-currant leaves and milk. My milk isn't sufficient for him.

May 19.

Misha is cutting his second tooth. He has four or five attacks a day of greenish diarrhœa, but he is fat and contented. He has milk with sugar and water through his rubber teat in the morning, and has his porridge at four. Miss Ford, the new English governess, has arrived. Varya (a girl of fifteen) takes Andryusha out for long walks, and is away nearly all day. She takes very good care of him. Misha sometimes chokes at the breast ; it's been happening for three weeks now.

January 27, 1881.

After dining and changing at the Khomyakovs, Tanya and I went to an amateur performance. I weaned Misha that day. He was a year old on December 20. He can stand alone now.

January 29.

Misha has started walking ; he took three steps to-day.

February 8, 1881.

Misha can now walk quite quickly about the drawing-room. He is cutting two lower back teeth. He already has ten teeth—eight in front and two upper back ones. I take Andryusha out every day for a walk or for a short sledge-drive. He can talk about anything now. He sleeps well, and hardly ever wakes, and doesn't have any more milk at night. He has stopped sleeping through the day. He has lunch at eleven in the forenoon, then he comes to my room and has a cup of tea and milk at twelve. He has dinner at four, a cup of tea and milk at eight, and then goes off promptly to be washed and put into his little bed. He is still wearing a girl's dress, and so does Misha.

[*Moscow*], *February 28, 1882.*

We've been in Moscow since September 15, 1881. We are staying in Prince Volkonsky's house, in the Denezhny Lane, near Prechistenka. Serezha has started going to the University. Tanya goes to a Miasnitskaya art school. Ilya and little Lyova go to Polivanov's high-school, which is next door to our house. Our life in Moscow would be very enjoyable if only it didn't make Lyova so unhappy. He is too impressionable for the life of a big city, and all this contrast of luxury and poverty, which one continually sees in a big town, doesn't seem to agree with his Christian moods. He went back to Yasnaya yesterday with Ilya, to do some work, and to have a rest.

August 26, 1882.

Twenty years ago, when I was a happy young woman, I started writing this book, the story of my love for Lyova. It deals with almost nothing else. And now, after twenty years, I am sitting up in the middle of the night, weeping over its loss. For the first time in my life Lyova has run away from me and has spent the night in his study. We quarrelled over mere trifles ; I blamed him for not taking a sufficient interest in the children, for not helping me to nurse Ilya, who is ill, or to make jackets for the children. But it isn't a question of jackets, it's a question of his increasing coldness towards me and the children. He cried out aloud to-day that his most passionate desire was to get away from his family. To my last breath shall I remember this candid exclamation, which seemed to tear out my heart. I am begging God to let me die, for I cannot live without his love ; I realised this the moment his love vanished. I can't tell him now how much I love him—it is the same love which I have given him all these twenty years. It humiliates *me* and annoys *him*. He is full of Christianity and the idea of self-perfection. I am jealous . . . Ilya has typhus ; he is lying in the drawing-room with a high fever ; I am careful to give him his quinine at the right intervals, which are short ones—so that I must be careful not to miss them. I shan't lie down on the bed which my husband has abandoned. God help me ! I want to kill myself—my thoughts are all confused. The clock is striking four. If he doesn't come back I shall know that he loves another woman. He hasn't come back. . . . My duty ? I've always known what my duty was. But what is my duty now ?

He came back, but we did not make peace until twenty-four hours later. We both wept, and I saw with joy that the old love, the loss of which I had bemoaned during all that dreadful night, was still alive in him. I shall never forget that lovely bright morning, with the silver dew sparkling on every leaf, when, after a sleepless night, I walked through the wood towards the bathing-cabin. I have seldom seen Nature in such triumphant beauty. I stayed for a long time in the ice-cold water, hoping to catch a chill and die. But

I did not catch a chill, and, instead, went home, and nursed my happy, smiling little Alyosha.

September 10, 1882.

Aunt Tanya and her family have gone off to Petersburg, and Lyova and little Lyova to Moscow. It has been the last warm day. I had a bathe.

Moscow, March 5, 1883.

The spring sun has always such an invigorating effect on me. It is shining so brightly through the window of my little study upstairs as I write ; and now, in the silence of the first week in Lent, I am going over in my mind all that I did during the past winter. I used to go out a little, enjoying Tanya's successes, and my own, thanks to my gaiety and youthfulness, and all the round of social pleasures. Yet who would believe that the moments of despair were more frequent than the moments of pleasure ; and in those gloomy moments I used to say to myself : "It is all wrong ; I am not doing the right thing." But I did not know how to stop—I *couldn't* stop, and it became increasingly clear to me that I was not responsible for my actions, but was compelled, even in small matters, to act as I was directed by God or Fate, or whatever else one may choose to call that superior power. The day before yesterday, or, rather, on the 2nd, I took Alyosha off the breast, and am once again feeling the same old grief of a first separation. And this grief comes back time and again, nor is there ever any escape. The life in our own house in this quiet part of the town is much happier and simpler than when we were in Moscow a year ago. Lyova is calm and contented, and his outbursts and reproaches are rarer and shorter than they used to be. He is becoming gentler every day.

But God knows, if no one else does, all that went on in my heart ; during last summer and autumn I did not want to go to Moscow, for I felt that all the weight and responsibility of the city life would be too much for me. I was leaving all that I loved in Yasnaya, and all that I was accustomed to. How I treasured it all after we came away, and yet we could have returned, even last year. . . . But this second moving is none of my doing—the father and the children arranged it between them. It was necessary, for it was God's wish to save the whole happiness of my family in this way. . . . But why ? Lyova is still busy writing in his Christian spirit, and this work will go on for ever, for it can never be printed. But it is necessary, and may be God will use it for His own great purposes.

March 24, 1885.

Holy Easter Sunday. Lyova came back from the Crimea yesterday, where he had gone with Urusov, who is seriously ill. There he remembered all about the Crimean War, and went for long mountain walks, and admired the sea. On their way to Simeiz, they passed the spot where Lyova had been stationed during the war, with his cannon, but he fired it only once. This is nearly thirty years ago. As Urusov and he drove along, he suddenly jumped out of the carriage and went to look for something ; it turned out that he had caught sight of a mountain artillery cannon-ball lying near the side of the road. Was it the ball that Lyova had fired during the Sebastopol campaign ? No one could have fired another one at that particular spot, then or at any other time. And there had been only *one* piece of mountain artillery. It is evening now; the elder children have gone out to the Olsufievs, and Lopatin[84] is singing to us.

Yasnaya Polyana, October 25, 1886.

Everyone, Lev Nikolaevich, as well as the children, who follow him like a flock of sheep—has come to think of me as a *scourge*. After throwing on me the whole responsibility of the children and their education, household duties, money matters, and all the other material things, which they all make much greater use of than I ever do, they come along, and, with a cold, officious, and pious expression, tell me to give a horse to a peasant, or some money, or some flour, or this, that, and the next thing.

I have nothing to do with the farming, and I have neither the time nor the knowledge to find out whether horses are required at one particular moment for a particular purpose, and all these requests, when I don't know what they are about, irritate and confuse me.

How often have I wanted to drop it all and to be done with this life. God ! I am so tired of all this life and the struggle and suffering ! How deep is the unconscious hatred of even one's nearest people, and how great their selfishness. But why am I going on with it all ? I don't know, and yet I believe it to be right. I shall never be able to do the things my husband wants (or says he wants), unless I can break all those family and business bonds, and all those emotional fetters in which I have lived for so long.

To get away, one way or another, from this house or out of this life, to leave all this cruelty, these impossible demands—that is the thought that is haunting me day and night. I have come to love the darkness. When it grows dark, I begin to feel happier, and my imagination begins to evoke the things I used to love, and I sit there, watching the phantoms. Last night I caught myself speaking aloud. I was so frightened : what if I am going mad ? And I love darkness nowadays—am I then to love death, too ?

For all its pain, these two months of Lev Nikolaevich's illness were, strangely enough, the last time of real happiness I have had. I nursed him day and night. It was such a happy, natural thing—the only thing I can do really well—to make a *personal* sacrifice for the man one loves. The harder it was, the happier it made me. Now he wanders about, and is nearly well. He has shown me clearly that he doesn't need me any longer, and now I am once again cast aside as of no further use, although I am, nevertheless, expected to do impossible things, like renouncing my property, giving up my convictions, and the education and welfare of my children—things which not only I, a sufficiently strong-minded woman, but a thousand others who firmly believe in this form of righteousness are incapable of doing.

We have already been in Yasnaya longer than usual. I am not strong enough to undertake anything. Yet my conscience is awake, and tells me that my energy is failing. I *must* follow the path which I know to be the right one, and yet I have lost all will-power. I shall probably have to go to Moscow again, still keep the family together, and have to handle all the publishing side, and to get all the money, which Lev Nikolaevich, with an injured air of indifference, is the first to ask for, and which he then distributes among his favourites and his poor, who aren't poor at all, but are merely more insolent than the others and better at begging from him. All those people like Constantine,[85] and Ganya,[86] and Alexander Petrovich,[87] and the rest. . . . The children, who have been blaming me for not siding with their father, are also expecting to get as much out of it as they can. . . . Oh, to get away from all this—and I shall—one way or another. I haven't sufficient strength left, nor do I care enough for it all, with its struggles and need for patience. I shall write my diary for the moment. It may make me kinder and more silent ; and perhaps all my excitement and irritation will be spent on it.

A bleak and dreary autumn. Andryusha and Misha went skating on the Lower Pond. Tanya and Masha have toothache. Lev Nikolaevich is planning to write a drama of peasant life. May God grant that he goes back to this kind of work ! His arm is aching with rheumatism. Mme. Seuron is a very pleasant woman and gets on well with the children. The boys—Serezha, Ilya, and Lyova—are going on with their mysterious life in Moscow ; I am very worried about them. They seem to have a strange attitude towards human passions and weaknesses—they consider them only natural and think they're very smart fellows if they overcome them. But why *must* there be these weaknesses ? I know that they do exist, and that *one* great effort will overcome them some day ; but what is the good of struggling with them daily ? The struggle is well worth it, though it sometimes ends in breaking your heart and life. But surely Strelna,* and drinking and gambling, and all those mean and vulgar little passions, aren't worth all that struggle.

I often wonder why Lyova is always making me out to be guilty, in spite of my innocence. No doubt because he wants to see me suffer at the sight of poverty and illness and misfortune, and actually *look* for it even if I have no opportunity of seeing it in my own surroundings—and he is expecting the same from the children. Is there any need for it ? Is there any need for a healthy human being constantly to keep going to hospitals to look at the sufferings and agony of the sick, and to listen to their groans ? If you come across a sick man in your own life, take pity on him and help him, by all means, but why go searching for him ?

I am reading the lives of the philosophers and am finding it extremely interesting. But it is hard for me to read it and keep calm and balanced. When I read these books, I keep looking for all the things that agree with my own views and convictions, and I skip over the rest. It is therefore hard for me to learn anything, though I am trying to be less partial.

Buturlin has come to stay with us. He is *genuine* ; there is no muddle about him.

October 26.

Lyova has written the first act of his play.[88] I am going to copy it out. Why have I lost my blind faith even in his literary power ? He has gone out for a stroll with Buturlin. It is damp and dark.

* A famous night restaurant.

I chattered too much to Buturlin, and forgot Epictetus's golden rule : *Garde le silence le plus souvent, ne dis que les choses nécessaires et toujours en peu de mots.* But Buturlin is intelligent and understands everything.

Andryusha and Misha are out playing with Mitrosha and Ilyukha, the peasant children. I don't know why, but I don't like it. It may be because it teaches them to rule over these children, which is wrong and immoral. Yesterday I read over some of Urusov's letters, and it is terrible to think that he is gone. I tried to find in them something that I always wanted to know even when he was alive : what were his feelings towards me ? There is one thing that I do know—that I always felt happy and cheerful when he was there ; but I don't know why he affected me in that way.

I keep thinking of the older boys—they seem to be so terribly far away from me, and it hurts me. Why don't things about children ever hurt fathers ? Why should women have to bear *this* weight also ? It only brings confusion into life.

I have copied the first act of Lyova's new play. It is very fine. The characters are marvellously drawn, and the plot is interesting and well arranged. I wonder what'll happen next. In the evening Lyova read his *Critique of Theology* to Buturlin. I listened to some of it, but kept thinking of other things. It has no effect on me ; is it wrong, or has my heart grown so cold and insensible ? A letter came from Ilya about his proposed marriage. I wonder if it isn't just the result of coming into close contact with a woman for the first time since he awakened to these things ? I can't make up my mind whether I want this marriage or not, and so, without taking any steps myself, I shall leave it all to God's decree. I coached Andryusha and Misha to-day, but with no interest or result. They are both very dear to me. I was correcting the proofs for the cheap edition, and am very tired. I am sorry to be leaving Yasnaya Polyana, especially as I don't want to see the work interrupted which Lyova has now begun. Masha runs about doing no work ; the boys give me much worry ; things aren't going at all well. My mind will be at rest if only Lyova settles down to work in Moscow. I shall be very careful and attentive to him and spare him as much as possible for the sake of his work, which I love so dearly.

October 30.

He has finished the second act of the play. I got up early to copy it out, and made a second copy in the evening. It is good, but too *even* ; he should put in a little more theatrical effect, and I told him so. I coached Andryusha and Misha and corrected some proofs, and was busy all day. I read *Home Echoes* and *The Fountain* to the little ones. They liked the pictures and the poems, and quite cheered up. Both the girls keep staying downstairs reading or writing. I had some moments of my old familiar feeling of sadness, and grew depressed. Aniska came to tell me of her mother's illness, but I was too lazy to go and see her, and must go to-morrow. At dinner they asked me for some money to give to some old woman, and that thief Ganya. The request was made by Lyova *via* the girls. I was hungry, and annoyed that everybody was late for dinner, and didn't want to give any money for the thief, and so, although I had a few roubles left, I told them I had no money. But later on I felt ashamed, and, after finishing my soup, I went and got some. (I only remembered about the soup afterwards.) After that, I was silent, and kept wondering whether it really was possible to feel that universal love, that Lyova expects, towards everybody and everything, even that thief, Ganya, who has robbed every single person in the village, who has a filthy disease, and is also most objectionable. For a second I seemed to feel sorry for her, but it soon passed. Feinemann[89] was here, too. His presence doesn't worry me as much as it used to. We had some letters from old Gé.[90] I don't feel I trust him—there is something false and affected about him.

Buturlin has left ; I am not sorry. And yet I found him interesting while he was here. Tanya reproached me nastily for not having given the money to her father. And for a second I really did feel that I hadn't given it to *him*, although he had asked for it. But I wasn't thinking of Lyova at the time. I knew the money wasn't for *him*, and I was unable to connect with him my refusal to give money to Ganya. This often happens to me.

Moscow, March 3, 1887.

We were very much perturbed by the news that four students in Petersburg had been found in possession of bombs, which they were going to throw at the Emperor while he was returning from his father's memorial service. I was so perturbed by it that I could think of nothing else all day. This evil will give birth to many more evils. Any kind of evil worries me terribly these days ! Lyova received the news sadly and silently ; he had already thought of it so often before.

The play is having an astounding success, but both Lyova and I are taking it calmly. I started writing my diary again at the time the play was begun, but had to give it up later, as there was so much copying to do. My mother died in Yalta on November 11, and was buried there. On the twenty-first I moved to Moscow with the family. Lyova has written a story about the early Christians, and is now working on an article " On Life and Death." He often complains of a pain in his side. We spent the winter peacefully and happily.

A new cheap edition has come out, but I have lost all interest in it. The money has brought me no joy—I knew it wouldn't. We have engaged a new English governess, Miss Fewson. Masha is ill. I was reading *King Lear* to her. I am fond of Shakespeare, though he is often brutal and untamed, especially in the endless murders and deaths in his plays.

March 6.

I copied out " On Life and Death," and read it over carefully. I tried hard to find something new in it ; but, although I found in it some shrewd remarks and some beautiful images, the central idea was still the same obvious one : the renouncement of the material, personal life in favour of the life of the spirit. There is one thing in all this which I find unjust and impossible—the idea that the personal life must be renounced in favour of a love for the whole world ;

I am sure that there are certain unquestionable duties which God has given us, and which no one has the right to renounce : they are not a hindrance, but a help to the life of the spirit.

I am feeling sad and weary. I am grieved at Ilya's shady and evil way of living. Idleness, vodka, much lying, bad company, and, above all, this complete absence of any spiritual life. Serezha has gone to Tula again ; there is a board meeting to-morrow at the Peasants' Bank. Tanya and Lyova have developed a deplorable passion for *vint*.* I seem to have lost all *educative* influence over the young ones. I feel terribly *sorry* for them, and am afraid to spoil them. I have a senile fear and a senile affection for them, and yet my desire to educate them on a sound basis remains as strong as ever. My life has lost its equilibrium, but I sometimes have some beautiful moments devoted to the solitary contemplation of death, when I clearly realise the duality of the physical and the spiritual consciousness, and the certain immortality of both.

Lyova often speaks of going back to the country, but in the end he always stays here. I keep quiet and feel I have no right to interfere with his actions. He has changed a great deal ; he looks at everything serenely and good-naturedly, and takes part in *vint*, or sits down to the piano. The town life doesn't seem to drive him to despair. We have a letter from Chertkov. I do not like him : he is clever and sly and one-sided, and is not a good man. L. N. is very partial to him because of his adulation. All the same, I admire and must do full justice to his popular books, which were originally L. N.'s idea. Feinemann[21] is in Yasnaya again. He

* A game resembling auction bridge.

has left his pregnant wife and his child in a penniless state, and has come to stay with us. I believe in the family principle, and to my mind he is worse than any man or beast. However fanatical his ideas may be, however beautiful his speeches, the monstrous fact remains that he has deserted his family and is making a living off other people's hospitality.

March 9, 1887.

Lyova is writing a new article, "On Life and Death," which is to be read to the Psychological Society at the University. Last week he again took up his vegetarianism, and it is already having an effect on his frame of mind. To-day he purposely started talking about the evils of wealth and money in front of me, and alluded to my desire to keep things for the children. I said nothing at first, but finally lost my temper and said: "I sell the twelve-volume edition for 8 roubles, while you used to charge 10 roubles for *War and Peace* alone." He grew angry, but said nothing. His so-called *friends*, the new Christians, try terribly hard to put L. N. against me—and are not always unsuccessful. I read over Chertkov's[90A] letter in which he spoke of the happy spiritual communion between himself and his wife, and expressed his sympathy and regret that such a worthy man as L. N. should be ignorant of such happiness and be deprived of such a *communion*—an obvious allusion to me. I read it over, and it hurt me. That blunt, sly, untruthful man, having succeeded in getting round L. N. with his flattery, is now trying (I suppose that's Christian) to destroy the bond which has so closely kept us together for nearly twenty-five years! The two months that Lev Nikolaevich was ill we spent in our good old way. I could see how his spirit was rested, and how all his old inspiration was coming back to him. He wrote his play then. But he is falling again into the snares of these false, sweet-mouthed, new Christians, and he is already wanting to go back to the country, and I can see the fire fading within him, and the effect of it all on his soul.

This relation with Chertkov must be put to an end. It is all false and evil, and we must get away from it.

We had visitors to-day—all young people. After dinner they played *vint*. What a sad thing this universal *vint* is! It is cold; fourteen degrees of frost at night.

Moscow, March 14, 1887.

I am quite alone; everything is silent, and I am feeling calm and happy. The three little ones are asleep. Tanya, Masha, and [young] Lyova have gone to the Tatishchevs. Ilya is locked up in the barracks for three days for being late for parade.[1] Lev Nikolaevich has gone with N. N. Gé (the son) to the University, where he is reading his paper "On Life and Death" to the Psychological Society. Gé[2] and I copied it out in a great hurry, and I was busy with it all day. L. N. is not feeling well; he has constant indigestion, and his diet is quite ridiculous; he eats rich food one day and vegetarian food the next, and rum and water and what not. He is depressed, but is kind. The Petersburg man, who was sent to Yasnaya Polyana for the costumes for our new play, has been here. I had a letter from Potekhin yesterday ; it still *isn't* certain that the play will be passed. All the same, it is being rehearsed, and all the preparations are on foot. I wonder if I should go to the dress rehearsal. I should like to, and yet I'm afraid to leave the house. I haven't quite decided yet ; it'll depend on Lyova's health. I took the children to the skating pond, but didn't skate myself. All the old pleasures are gradually disappearing. Lyova has been working hard on his article, with which he is very pleased. This is his second visit to the University. He has been breaking some of his silly rules of late. Grigori often does his room now, and when he is not feeling well he eats meat, and when we play *vint* he sits down to it too. Some of his obstinacy and his bad moods seem to have gone, and he has become kinder and more cheerful. He has also stopped objecting to the sale of the books, and is quite glad that they are 8 roubles a set.

March 30, 1887.

Lyova's health is still poor. The pain in his side has been going on for three months. I decided to get Zakharyin to come and see him, and wrote him a note, but before he came L. N. went yesterday to see him himself. Zakharyin found that he had catarrhal jaundice, and prescribed the following (I am writing from memory) :

(1) To wear warm clothes.
(2) To wear unbleached flannel round the waist.
(3) Not to eat butter.
(4) Eat often, and only a little at a time.
(5) Take half a tumbler of fresh Ems Kränchen or Kesselbrunn three or four times a day—(*a*) on an

empty stomach ; (*b*) an hour before and quarter of an hour after lunch ; and (*c*) one hour before dinner. To do this for three weeks without a break, and then stop, and begin again later, if necessary. It must be taken as warm as he can drink it without burning himself—warmer than new milk.

(6) Cut down smoking, as much as possible.

June 18, 1887.

Many people blame me for not writing my diary and memoirs, since Fate has put me in touch with such a famous man. But it is so hard to break away from my *personal* attitude towards him, to be quite impartial, and, most of all, to find any time to do it ; I am so terribly busy, and it's been the same all my life. I thought I would be free enough this summer to copy and sort out some of Lev Nikolaevich's manuscripts. But I've been here a whole month now, and have had to spend all this time copying " On Life and Death," on which he has worked for such a long time.

No sooner am I finished copying it than he changes it all, and I have to copy it all over again. His patience and determination are endless. I really ought to write my memoirs, if only to explain so many obscure things about his life. For instance, there is his letter to Engelhardt, numerous written copies of which are being handed round ; L. N. has never even met young Engelhardt, who, like many other people, wrote to L. N., because he was a famous author. But L. N. was in a gloomy mood that day. Having expressed certain ideas in his writings, he was unable to apply them in practice, and, feeling miserable and depressed because of it, he poured forth all his thoughts in this letter to a stranger, just as if it were a diary.[93]

Much stranger still are his relations and his correspondence with people who are simply dishonourable, and whose reputation is terrible—as, for instance, Ozmidov. The other day I saw Ozmidov's name written on an envelope, and asked Lev Nikolaevich why he was still continuing this correspondence, even though he knew quite well that Ozmidov was an evil man. " If he is an evil man," he replied, " I can be of greater help to him than to anybody else." This explains his relations with many wicked and insignificant people, some of them obscure strangers, who flock to see us in large numbers. Yesterday a fourth-year medical student, a violent revolutionary, called, and Lev Nikolaevich spent his time explaining to him the fallacy, harm, and uselessness of revolution. I don't know whether he convinced him or not ; I saw no signs of it. To-day we got several letters from America, and the *Century*, with Kennan's[94] article on his visit to Yasnaya Polyana and his talks with Lev Nikolaevich, and a review of L. N.'s translated works—all very flattering and sympathetic. It is strange and pleasant to find such sympathy and appreciation so many thousands of miles away.

Lyova has gone to Yasenki, walking, with his two daughters and the two Kuzminsky girls. As it began to rain, I sent the carriage and some coats after them. Without his apostles, Chertkov, Feinemann, and the rest, Lyova is once again the same happy, joyful father of the family. The other day he spent the whole evening playing Mozart, Weber, and Haydn, and one could see how much he was enjoying it. The violin part was played by a youth of eighteen whom Lyova had engaged as a teacher for [young] Lyova. The latter had been wanting to learn the violin. This youth, Liassota by name, is a student of the Moscow Conservatoire. When I arrived in Moscow on May 11, I firmly asked Lyova to take the water that Zakharyin had prescribed ; and he submitted. Without saying a word, I used to take him a glass of warm Ems, which he would drink in silence. When he was in a bad mood, he would say : " If anyone tells you to pour something into me, you at once believe that it *must* be done. I'm only taking it because it can't do me much harm, anyway." But, all the same, he kept it up for the three weeks and did not go back to his vegetarian diet, and, in my opinion, his health has greatly improved. He walks a great deal and has become stronger, but he has only seven hours sleep—which I don't think is enough. But this may be due to his lack of exercise.

The success, or rather the response he has got from America, is giving him great joy, although usually success and fame make no great impression on him. He is looking happy and full of energy, and often says : " Life is a fine thing."

I am missing Ilya, and am worried not to have gone to see him yet. But during this past year he has been showing so little interest in the family that I don't suppose he really wants us. The poor boy seems to have got lost, to have deteriorated in the moral sense, and that may be why he looks so miserable and wretched. I must go and see him one of these days.

Crowds of sick people come to see me every day. I treat them all in accordance with Florinsky's book ; but it is mental agony when you don't know what kind of disease it is, and how it can really be helped. That is why I sometimes feel like giving it all up, but when I go out and see their touching faith, and imploring eyes, I begin to feel sorry, and, although it grieves me to think that I am doing the wrong thing, I hand out the medicine—and then try to forget all about the poor devils. The other day, I hadn't the right medicine, and so gave the woman some money and a note to take to the chemist. But she gave me back the money, and, beginning to cry, said : " I am sure to die, so take the money, and give it to someone poorer than me ; thank you all the same, but I don't need it."

June 21.

It is hot at last, and I have had my first bathe. Andreyev-Burlak, the actor, came last night to make L. N.'s acquaintance, and told us stories of peasant life in the amusing Gorbunov manner. After the others had gone to bed, Lev Nikolaevich, Lyova, and I stayed up listening to his stories till two in the morning. His stories were wonderful, and Lev Nikolaevich laughed so much that Lyova and I got quite nervous. He spent the morning correcting his article " On Life and Death," and after dinner went out to mow the grass in the garden. I read Strakhov's book against spiritualism ; it is difficult to read, and, alas, not convincing —or perhaps I can't understand it. In the afternoon, before bathing, I gathered the young ones round me and read *A Hero of our Times* to them. I found some wonderful, fully matured thoughts in it. I love Lermontov. Even if, as rumour has it, he was an irritable, disagreeable person, he was so intelligent and so very far above the ordinary human level. People didn't understand him, while he was able to see right through everybody.

I am feeling weak, both physically and mentally. I am depressed with so many thoughts and regrets about the past, and what can be worse than that?

July 2, 1887.

I have been to Moscow to see Ilya. I was so glad to see his good-natured face again; and I could see he was glad to see me too. He lives in a hut, and his landlords seem to like him, only he lives in such an untidy way! I, who had fed him at my breast, felt sad that he should have to spend the money I sent him paying off his debts, and be forced to get sweets and knick-knacks on credit, and never have any dinner at all. But he doesn't seem to mind. His whole interest in life is Sonya Filosofov.•• He lives entirely on memories, letters, and future plans. He is here now; he was out shooting, killed three snipe, and is leaving to-morrow. It is very sad to see the fledglings leave the nest; but I'll have to get used to it.

Strakhov•• is staying with us. What a good-natured, gentle, and clever man! Lyova is busy mowing the grass, and spends three hours a day on his article. It's coming to an end now. The other night Serezha was playing a waltz, when Lyova came up to me, saying: "Let us do a round." This we did, to the great delight of all the young people. He is very cheerful and lively, but he is weaker, and gets more easily tired after his walks and the mowing. He has long talks on science, art, and music with Strakhov; to-day they talked about photography, as I had brought back a camera, with which I intend to take pictures and family groups. My daughter Tanya has gone to Pirogovo.

July 3.

Serezha and Liassota, the violinist, are playing Beethoven's Kreutzer Sonata. What a powerful work, expressing as it does every possible human emotion ! There are roses and resedas standing on my table, and we are going to have such a fine dinner. The weather is warm and still after the storm, and my children are so lovely ; Andryusha has just been busy upholstering the chairs in the nursery ; and soon my kind and beloved Lyova will come back—such is my life that I am consciously revelling in and for which I offer God my thanks. I find *happiness* and *the Good* in all these things. And now I am copying Lyova's article " On Life and Death," and it points to quite a different Good. When I was very, very young, before I was married, I remember aiming at that *other* Good—complete self-renunciation, the devotion of my life to others, even asceticism. But Fate gave me a family, to whom I have devoted my life, and now I am asked to admit that it isn't right, that it isn't *life*. Shall I ever come to see it in that light ?

Strakhov went away yesterday, and Ilya to-day. Serezha and I experimented with the camera which I brought from Moscow.

July 19, 1887.

We have had a few disturbed days. Serezha came back from Samara, where he didn't manage to get anything done. We had a visit from P. D. Golokhvastov,[1] an extreme Orthodox and Slavophil; he and Lev Nikolaevich had long talks on religion and the Church. It was very unpleasant. Golokhvastov spoke with great pathos about the marvellous cathedral in New Jerusalem (Voskresensk), which is wonderfully built and can hold ten thousand people. L. N. listened for a long time, and then suddenly said : " They all go there to have a laugh at God." He said it ironically, even spitefully. I broke into the conversation, saying that it showed too much pride, on his part, to say that 10,000 people were wrong and he alone right in his belief, and that he must admit that there must have been a more sublime motive than mockery which took those ten thousand people into the church.

Butkevich has been here ; he is a former revolutionary who has been in jail, once for political offences and the next time on suspicion. He is a young man, the son of a Tula landowner. He wrote to Lev Nikolavich saying that soon after he was released from prison a lady he had known cut him dead in the street —which caused him much pain at the time. When he used to come to see L. N., I never invited him to stay, and he remained in the study, but this time I felt sorry for him and asked him to tea. Then he stayed on for two days, and I took a great dislike to him. He is very solemn, with a stony expression, very dark hair, blue spectacles, and a squint. One can't make anything of the few words he utters. He has now become a *Tolstoist.* What disagreeable characters, all these disciples of Lev Nikolaevich are ! Not a single sane person among them ! Most of the women are hysterical. Marie Alexandrovna Schmidt has just left.

In the old days she would have been a nun ; now she is an enthusiastic worshipper of Lev Nikolaevich's ideas ! She used to be a schoolmistress at the Nicholas Institute, but left because she deserted the Church, and now she is staying in the village, making a living by copying Lev Nikolaevich's prohibited works. Every time she meets him or says good-bye she weeps hysterically. Pavel Nikolaevich Birukov is here, too : I still prefer him to the rest ; he is gentle and clever, and also professes Tolstoism. In addition, Golokhvastova has arrived with her pupil, and my nephew Andryusha with his tutor.

It is very noisy and tiring. I long for some of the intimacy of the family circle, and a more orderly existence, as regards both work and recreation. The visitors are taking up all my time. The Abameleks were here too, and brought the Helbigs, mother and daughter with them ; her maiden-name is Princess Shakhovskoy, and she is married to a German professor ; she and her daughter also came to see that Russian celebrity—Tolstoy. Although they were quite nice people and good musicians, I find it very trying *not* to be able to choose my friends and to have to receive anybody and everybody. It is hot in the daytime, but cool at night. We go bathing. There is a lot of fruit this summer.

August 4, 1887.

Countess Alexandra Andreyevna Tolstoy left to-day, after having been here since July 25. Lyova had a severe bilious attack on July 16, and he has been feeling liverish ever since ; he has been having pain in his side again, and constipation and cloudy urine. Last night, Birukov[11] took his article "On Life" to the printers. The words "and Death" have been left out. After finishing the article he decided that *there was no death.* It has been raining, but has cleared up now.

August 19, 1887.

Repin, the painter, has been here. He arrived on the ninth and left on the night of the sixteenth. He painted two portraits of Lev Nikolaevich ; he began the first one in the study, but wasn't satisfied with it and started on another one, with a light background, in the drawing-room. The portrait is wonderful. It is still here drying. He finished off the first one quickly and made me a present of it. They started printing the article, but the type is bad and they'll have to re-set it. Lyova's health is fairly good, though he still sometimes complains of his liver. The weather is lovely. Ilya came down for the fifteenth and sixteenth ; he is well and in high spirits—and that is always something to be thankful for. Some useless people manage to be gloomy and ill as well ! My pregnancy is troubling me both physically and morally. Lyova is losing his health, our family life is becoming more and more complicated, and I am losing my moral strength. My brother Stepa and his wife came here. She has stayed on, while he has gone to Petersburg to see if they will transfer him to European Russia. I can't make her out ; she is very reserved and tries to make herself useful about the house. Lyova has his "dark" people with him — Butkevich, Rakhmanov, and an undergraduate, Kievsky—a disagreeable lot of strangers, very depressing and unbearable in our family circle. And there are so many of them! It's a heavy price to pay for Lyova's fame and new ideas.

In the evening he reads Gogol's *Dead Souls* to us. I have neuralgia.

August 25.

I spent all day looking through Lyova's manuscripts, and sorting them out. I want to take them to the Rumiantsev Museum to be preserved. Some of them are in a dreadful muddle, and, I am sure, will never be deciphered or completed. I also want to take his letters, diaries, portraits, and everything else relating to him. I am acting in a *sensible* way, but for some reason it makes me sad. Does my desire to put everything in order mean that I shall soon die?

Stepa,[88] his wife, and that charming Strakhov are here just now. The heat is terrific, and I have a sore throat. Lyova is feeling run-down and started taking Ems again on the twentieth. Vera Tolstoy and Masha have arrived to get some money for Serezha (Lyova's brother). Lyova is working on his article, but his energy seems to have disappeared for this kind of work.

Lev Nikolaevich began taking Ems Kesselbrunn on June 17, 1888.

He took the same water for four weeks in June 1889, and for four more weeks in May 1890. He drank kumyss all that summer.

[*A pressed flower glued to the Diary at this point.*]

Lyova gave me this flower at Yasnaya Polyana in October 1890.

Yasnaya Polyana, November 20, 1890.

I am busy copying Lyova's diary, which he has been writing all his life and I have decided to take up my *own* diary once again ; especially as I have never felt more lonely in the midst of my own family than now. My children are scattered—Serezha at Nikolskoye, Ilya and his family at Grinevka, [young] Lyova in Moscow, and now Tanya has gone to join him for some time. Masha and I never felt particularly fond of one another ; I don't know whose fault it is. Probably mine. Lyova has broken off all relations with me. Why ? What for ? I can't understand it. When he is ill, he takes it for granted that I must look after him, but even then he is gruff and unfriendly, and needs me only so long as he needs his poultices, enemas, etc. I have tried with all my heart to attain to some degree of spiritual communion with him.

I read his diaries on the quiet, and tried to see what I could bring into his life which would unite us again. But his diaries only deepened my despair ; he evidently discovered that I had been reading them, for he hid them away. However, he didn't say anything to me.

In the old days it gave me joy to copy out what he wrote. Now he keeps giving it to his daughters and carefully hides it from me. He makes me frantic with his way of systematically excluding me from his personal life, and it is unbearably painful. This unfriendly existence at times drives me to the depths of despair. I feel like killing myself or running away, or falling in love with someone—anything to escape from a man whom, in spite of everything, for some unknown reason, I have loved all my life, although

I now see clearly that I idealised him, without realising that there was nothing in him except sensuality . . .* But now he has opened my eyes for me, and I see that my life has been wasted. How envious I am now even of such people as the Nagornyis ; for, after all, they are *together*—there is some other link between them besides the mere physical one. Many other people live like that. As for us—good God, it is sufficient to hear his cold, irritable, insincere tone when he is talking to me. To think that he can talk like that to me, when I am so joyful, candid, and so eager for affection ! I am going to Moscow to-morrow on business. I find it always very hard and exhausting, but I am glad to be going this time. These hard times are like the ebb and flow of the sea ; and when I begin to realise my solitude, I want to weep and to put an end to it—it would be easier then. It has become my habit to pray at much length every evening ; it is a good way to finish the day. I was teaching Andryusha and Misha music to-day, and was angry all the time. Andryusha takes my bad temper peevishly, but I always feel sorry for Misha. I love them very much, and the task of educating them is a pleasant duty to me, though, no doubt, I do it badly and inefficiently. Vera Kusminsky is staying with us ; I feel a motherly affection for her—probably because she reminds me of her mother, my sister Tanya. I am glad to live in the country, and the solitude and restfulness of Nature gives me much pleasure. If only *someone* had more sympathy for me ! Sometimes, for days, weeks, and even months on end, we hardly exchange a word. As a matter of habit, I run up to him with my own

* Sixty-five words missing.

thoughts and concerns—the children, or a book, or anything at all—but he meets me with a cold, surprised, forbidding look, as much as to say: "You are still hopeful, and keep on bothering me with your nonsense." Is a bond of sympathy still possible between us? Or is all dead? I often wish I could go up to his study and once again look through his papers and diaries, and discuss everything with him; it would help me to live. Even if he would speak from his heart, as he used to, and not so unnaturally as he does now—that alone would be something to be thankful for. But now, though I am innocent, and love him and have never done him the slightest injury during all his life, I feel like a criminal and am afraid of him. I fear that cold, forbidding, unloving look of his, which is more painful than any words or blows. He never knew how to love—it is something he never *learned* in his youth.

December 5, 1890.

I am going on with my diary. I was up in Moscow, where I saw many people and found much friendliness. It's always something to be thankful for. Tanya was there; her company always cheers me, and I treasure her intimacy. Lyova's state of moral jumpiness is still the same, and it hurts me each time I go near him, but at least he is aware of it each time he hurts me. I wonder when he'll get out of his nervous state of pessimism.—I came back on the morning of the twenty-fifth. Lyova was on the point of going to Krapivna with Masha, Vera Tolstoy, and Vera Kusminsky. It was cold and there was a blizzard, but, all the same, I was unable to dissuade them from going. There was a trial on, and, thanks to Lyova's intervention, the murderers got off with a very light sentence. Instead of penal servitude, they were only condemned to deportation. So Lyova and the girls returned home in a very cheerful state. Misha had high fever for five days ; there was something wrong with his stomach. I had to take very great care of him, which was very tiring immediately after my Moscow journey. —We have more visitors : the sick Rusanov, Boulanger, Butkevich, and Petya Rayevsky. Except for the last one, they are all strangers, and they bore me. Lyova and I are more friendly these days, but everything depends on his moods with him. To-day I played Beethoven's Sonata *una fantasia* and his Adelaide, and tried over some Schubert. In the evening I read some of Fet's poems to the visitors to keep them amused, though I enjoyed both the music and the poetry too. Tanya and Masha went to see Vera Kusminsky off to Tula, and came back for dinner. I went to Tula yesterday also, to see about the sale of timber, and about my case against the Ovsiannikovo priest, to deposit money at the bank, and to do some shopping. After spending all my energy on these practical matters, I always feel depressed and annoyed. I could spend it on so many other things.

December 6.

It's a public holiday, and Andryusha's thirteenth birthday. We all went up the hill, and then went skating. The young village folks were all in their Sunday best. The children enjoyed themselves thoroughly.

I skated in a very slovenly way—it doesn't seem to amuse me any longer. Tanya went to Tula to the name-day parties at the Davydovs and Zinovievs. We still have the same visitors—Rusanov, Boulanger, Butkevich, and Petya Rayevsky, whom Tanya took with her to Tula. I feel I am degenerating physically. My chest is sore, and I have difficulty in breathing, and my condition is painful and nerve-racking. I got a letter which made me very happy from Sophie Alexeyevna Filosofov[100] about my elder sons; everything appears to be all right with them. Mothers have only one desire in life—that their children should be *happy*. Lyova is very cold and reserved with everybody, but I feel it most of all. I haven't done much work; I copied a little from Lev Nikolaevich's diaries, entertained the visitors, and worried about the children. Vanya[101] is taking up much of my time.

December 7.

I've been writing all day, and I'm not feeling well. Davydov called, with a magistrate, on their way to Krapivna. I read Leskov's tale, *One Godly Hour*. Very good, but artificial. I dislike artificiality in everything. Lyova is in a good mood, and seems to be well.

December 8.

I am going on copying Lyova's diary. I wonder why I've never read or copied it before; it has been in one of my drawers for such a long time; I don't think I have ever got over all the horror I experienced when I read Lyova's diaries before our marriage, and I doubt that the sharp sting of jealousy and my bewilderment at the thought of such filth and debauchery, has ever quite disappeared. May God preserve all young souls from such wounds—for they will never heal. I gave Misha and Andryusha their music lesson in the morning. Andryusha was so naughty and obstinate that I nearly lost my temper. But I stopped myself in time, and, instead of scolding him, I burst into tears. He began to cry also, and promised to work better—which, indeed, he did at once. I felt ashamed, but, after all, it may be for the best. I read a silly story in the *Revue des Deux Mondes*, and in the evening Lyova asked Tanya to read a translation of a very dull Swedish story. I wish I could read something important, something philosophic, but I can't decide on anything. I am in a good frame of mind now, and only want to think of pleasant things. But my dreams are sinful, and I feel very restless, especially sometimes.

Sunday, December 9.

Once again I have a heavy heart at the end of the day. Everything is worrying me. I was copying Lyova's old diary . . .* It was a lovely day, so I went for a walk and thought over so many things. It was fourteen below zero, and very clear, with the snow hanging heavily on the shrubs and trees. I went towards the young wood, past the haystacks ; the sun was setting to the left and the moon rising on the right. The sky was blue above the white tops of the trees which shone with a pale rosy light, and further on, in the meadow, the snow was spotlessly white. There was real *purity.*

* Twenty-eight words left out.

Purity is beautiful anywhere and in anything—in nature, in the souls and consciences of men, in morals, and in the material life—everywhere. But why did I try so hard to preserve it? Would not the remembrance of even a criminal love be better than my purity of conscience—and this awful sense of void?

I played Mozart's Symphony; at first with Tanya, and then with Lyova. It didn't go very well with him at first and he growled at me—but it was only for a moment and was hardly noticeable; but this tone of his has worried me for so long that it at once destroyed all my pleasure in playing with him. I grew sad—terribly sad. Burukov's arrival interrupted our playing. The girls grew excited—Tanya for Masha's sake, and Masha for her own sake. Everybody became formal—and, though we all talked a great deal, it was all strained and unnatural. I hope he goes away soon, so that Masha can calm down again. But, once a silly affair has been started, it isn't so easy to stop it. I read a novel in the *Revue des Deux Mondes*. There's a bit in it about a girl who goes to see the man she loves, and who feels happy to be surrounded by the things amongst which he lives. How very true!

But if these things are merely dirt and boots and shoemaker's tools, and chamber pots—what then? No, I shall never get used to it.[102]

December 10, 1890.

What sad times have come to me in my old age. Lyova has picked up a crowd of very queer new friends who call themselves his followers. This morning one of them arrived—a certain Butkevich, wearing black spectacles, and looking all black and mysterious, who had been exiled to Siberia for his revolutionary ideas—and he brought his mistress along with him, a Jewess to whom he referred as his wife, merely because he happened to be living with her. As Birukov, was there too, Masha went down and talked very pleasantly to the Jewess. It annoyed me terribly that a decent girl, and my daughter at that, should mix with such rabble, and that her father actually seemed to approve ! I lost my temper and began to scream, and, remembering all the painful things I had read when copying his diaries . . .* said angrily to him: "You have been used to disreputable company all your life, but I am *not* used to it and I won't have my daughters mix with them." As usual, he sighed, and growing angry, walked away without saying anything. Birukov's presence is so depressing ; I'm counting the hours till his departure. Masha stayed alone in the drawing-room with him last night, and I thought that he was kissing her hand. When I told her she grew angry and denied it. Maybe she is right—but who can make head or tail of anything in this lying, false, unhealthy atmosphere ? I am quite exhausted, and sometimes I wish I could get rid of Masha, and I ask myself: " Why am I trying to keep her back ? Let her marry Birukov by all means, for I can then once again take my place beside Lyova and do his copying for him and put his papers and letters in order, and gradually get him away from this hateful world of " the dark ones."

[Young] Lyova hasn't come back yet ; I wonder how he is. Andryusha, Misha, and I talked about acting a

* Four words missing.

play after Christmas, based on a Japanese fairy-tale. I have been knitting a blanket for Misha, and have been copying and teaching them scripture for two hours, and am now going to do some reading.

December 11.

I have been copying Lyova's diary ever since morning, and it always brings so many thoughts to my mind. It occurred to me, for instance, that you can't really love someone who knows you intimately, with all your weaknesses, and to whom you can't only show one side of the medal. That's why married people drift apart in their old age—i.e. when no further illusions are left, and everything is too obvious to be hidden from either of them. I taught them music patiently and well. Birukov has stayed on for another day. Masha came to talk over yesterday's incident with me, and I told her I was sorry if I accused her wrongly. By the way, she said, with a flippant laugh : " Let me marry him and put an end to it. Didn't you say he was a good man ? " As if that alone were enough. I have noticed that if mothers have a certain degree of infatuation for their future sons-in-law, the marriages always turn out to be successful.* [Young] Lyova has come back, and I suddenly felt in a holiday mood ; but, like his father, he was gloomy and was mainly taken up with himself. Vanichka was so glad to see him and looked at him so affectionately, and yet he merely frowned at the child. That's how one stamps out all feelings of love and friendliness, in children as well as in grown-ups. When [little] Lyova

* Twenty-five words left out.

as a delicate child was taken away from his English governess and handed over to a tutor, he wept and kept on saying that he wanted to go back, and that it would *spoil* him. But his father wouldn't hear of it; and, heaven knows, this harshness may have been the cause of a certain lack of affection and spontaneity and strength of character in the boy. We spent the evening together. Tanya has a pain in her back and is strangely silent. Here is a girl who needs a change and a family of her own. I pray for it every day. I wondered to-day if it wasn't really a sin to grumble against Fate so much; for, though a certain part of my happiness is lost, there is still much left, and I can still say with all my heart: "I thank thee, O Lord."

At dinner Lyova said that the peasants, who had cut thirty birch-trees and against whom proceedings had been taken, were waiting for me outside. Every time somebody is waiting for *me*; It is always *I* who have to decide everything.[10] I get terrified and want to weep; I feel as though I had been caught in a trap, and the task of running this *Christian* household is still the greatest curse that God has sent me. If spiritual salvation consists in killing the life of your neighbour, then Lyova is surely saved. But is it not, after all, death for both of us?

December 13.

I didn't write anything yesterday; I was so upset all day about the peasants who were being tried; but no news arrived that day. Birukov has gone, and Dillon, the English translator of *Walk in the Light*, etc., has arrived. I spent the day copying the diary of Lyova's youth; and at times I felt sorry for him—he was so lonely and helpless in those days. But all his life he has followed the same path—the path of thought. To-day I learned that the peasants were sentenced to six weeks imprisonment and a fine of twenty-seven roubles. I had spasms in my throat again, and felt like weeping all day long. I felt so sorry for *myself*; why should people be punished in *my* name, when I wish no one any evil. Even from the legal point of view, none of it is my property, and yet I have to play the part of a *scourge*. I coached the children for three hours on end without losing patience. Lyova and I had a talk about Tanya and Masha yesterday, and we both want to see them married, though certainly not to Birukov. I see very little of Lyova; being left alone seems to have a happy and quietening effect upon him, though it makes me so sad and depressed that I sometimes don't desire to live any longer.

Tanya, Masha, Lyova, Lizzie, Andryusha, and Misha went out late in the evening to the ice mountain with their sledges, while Lyova and I looked on. It was a glorious moonlit night, fifteen below zero; the brilliantly white snow and the trees, were so beautiful in the moonlight that one could hardly tear oneself away. I said to Lyova: "To keep looking at this is all one needs." But he replied: "It isn't enough for me."

December 14.

I copied Lyova's diaries up to where he says: "*There is no love, there is only the physical craving for intercourse and the rational need of a life companion.*" If only I had read this opinion twenty-nine years ago,

I should never have married him . . .* The day went past in the usual way : I coached Misha, looked after Vanichka, and had a talk with Dillon. A. V. Zinger, a student, has arrived. I taught Sasha the Lord's Prayer, and hadn't much time left for copying. I talked to Masha about Birukov. She said that she will either marry him or, if I object, refuse to marry at all. But she added later on, " But don't worry. All kinds of things may happen." It struck me as though she would be only too glad to get rid of these casual ties. She and Tanya had some mysterious talks together and seemed to enjoy themselves. I have written several letters—to my sister Tanya, to a French paper about an article in the *Figaro* of November 21, 1890, on the profits I make from the foreign editions of Lev Nikolaevich's works, to Dunayev and A. A. Behrs.

December 15.

A stupid kind of day. Our music lesson was interrupted by the arrival of Sytin, whom Tanya had asked to come about the Yasnaya school. Bulygin came for dinner. I took the children out twice. The second time, in the evening, I took out Sasha, who found it *boring* to stay indoors. There is a feeling of moral depression weighing on everybody and everything in the house. As a result of the sentence passed on the Yasenki peasants Lyova is more gloomy and depressed than ever. When it was discovered and the constable came to the house, I asked Lyova what to do and whether we should take any action. He thought about it for a while, and then said : " We

* Twenty-eight words left out.

must give them a fright, but forgive them afterwards." Then it turned out to be a criminal case, so that we were no longer in a position to forgive them, and, of course, it is *my* fault now. He is angrily silent, and I don't know what he is going to do about it ; as for me, I am sick and weary of the whole affair.[103] I've been seriously thinking of going once again to see Ilya, saying good-bye to everybody, and then lying down on the railway line—a threat that Agafya Mikhailovna so often liked to make. But I'm frightened and it's more easily said than done. Dillon[104] left this morning, and Bulygin and Zinger in the evening, so that we have no visitors with us now.

December 16, 1890.

Yes, I have lost all power to concentrate on any thought, feeling, or action. This chaos of endless worries, stumbling over each other, drives me to a state of complete bewilderment and I lose all my balance. The very thought of all these things, which take up every moment of my life, is overwhelming—children's lessons and illnesses, my husband's physical and, above all, his mental state, the older children, with all their affairs, and debts and posts and children, the sale of the Samara estate, the plans and documents I have to obtain and copy for the purchasers, the new edition, the thirteenth volume, which contains the banned Kreutzer Sonata, the proceedings against the Ovsiannikovo priest, the proof of volume thirteen, nightshirts for Misha, sheets and shoes for Andryusha, household expenses, insurance, land taxes, servants' passports, accounts to be kept and copied, etc., etc., etc. Every single one of these things has got to be looked after. And when something goes wrong like that business with the peasants, I suddenly realise that I have been at fault and that I have lost something of my strength—that I have hurt Lyova against my will. When we lodged our complaint with the rural court, we were determined to forgive them after the sentence was passed. But no, the case turned out to be a *criminal* one ; the sentence could not be changed, and Lyova is nearly driven to despair that the Yasenki peasants have been sent to jail because of *his* property.[10] He could not sleep at night, and jumped out of bed, and kept pacing up and down the drawing-room, gasping for breath, and, of course, blaming me—and in a very cruel way. I did not lose my temper, thank heaven, for I knew all the time that he was a sick man ; but what greatly astonished me was that he was trying to make me pity him ; but at the same time he never once made any effort to see my point of view and to understand that I had never intended to hurt either him or the thievish peasants. This self-adoration comes out in every one of his diaries. It is amazing how people existed for him only in so far as they affected him personally. And the women ! I caught myself up to-day on an evil thought. I copy his diaries with the zest of a drunkard, and my drunkenness consists in working myself up into a state of jealousy over the women he describes . . .* I am still restless and cannot shake off those memories. Never. . . . Another thing in his diaries strikes me as curious—the fact that, simultaneously with his daily debauches, he also tried *to do a good deed* every day. And now, too, when he goes for his walks on the high-road, he will show a drunken man the way,

* Thirty-two words missed out.

help to harness a horse, or pull a cart out of the ditch —it is still a case of looking *for good deeds*. It is Sunday to-day, and, after a dreary night of reproaches and arguments, my heart feels as heavy as a stone. The day dragged past wearily. There was a snowstorm, and only the boys went out. [Young] Lyova wanted to go and see Ilya, but turned back after passing the village. In the evening we read a French translation of Chinese fairy-tales. Very quaint. I played the piano for a little. Vanya and Sasha danced, and the general atmosphere cheered up a little as time went on.

December 17.

All the harshness and indifference has melted away and has resolved itself in the usual thing . . .* It is beginning to worry him that I have been copying his diaries . . .† He would like to destroy his old diaries and to appear before his children and the public only in his patriarchal robes. His vanity is immense !

The " dark " ones have arrived : Popov,[105] that inane and stupid Asiatic, and that fat fool of a Khokhlov,[106] of shopkeeper origin. And those are the followers of a great man ! Miserable abortions of human society, aimless babblers, uneducated loafers ! Tanya and [young] Lyova have gone to see Serezha and Ilya. I stayed at home, as I didn't feel well, and hadn't slept. Our lessons were interrupted by the arrival of E. E. Kern, a former forester on the Zaseka crown forest, and now a landowner. He gave me some very useful advice and information about forestry and gardening . . .‡

* Forty-six words left out. † Nine words left out.
‡ Thirty-two words left out.

December 19, 1890.

Yesterday morning I went to Tula with Andryusha and M. Borel. It was very cold, and I felt worried about Andryusha. We rushed round shopping and giving orders, and dropped in for a moment to see the Rayevskys, but found only the boys at home. We got back in time for dinner. In the evening Alexander Mitrofanovich read us a long, dreary story about the German colonies, and we looked through the *Review of Reviews*. I was tired and restless, and Popov and Khokhlov got on my nerves with their colourless, ineffectual silence . . .*

I got up late this morning, as I hadn't slept, and found Zhirkevich in the drawing-room, a smart young officer who had come to make Lyova's acquaintance. He writes prose and poetry himself; he is evidently very well pleased with himself and his position, but he is quite intelligent and talkative—not like the "dark" ones. I took Vanichka for a walk—it is the first time in winter. Sasha went with us. I taught Misha some prayers and the New Testament, and now I am writing my diary, after copying only two pages of Lyova's, although my usual daily rate is ten. I was dissatisfied with Andryusha; he sometimes *deliberately refuses* to understand, and doesn't make the slightest mental effort. In the evening I shall have to entertain the visitor, read for a while, and then have a bath.

December 20, 1890.

I didn't sleep, and got up late. I am in a terrible state of nervous excitement and have much pain in

* Thirty-five words missing.

my back. I went skating with the children, but was afraid of falling ; the ice was very poor ; then the children and I shovelled snow with the gardener and some village girls, and later I gave Sasha her first skating lesson. After coming home, I coached the children for three hours—Andryusha, in the Church service and both of them in music. It is Misha's eleventh birthday. Lyova came back from seeing Ilya, and brought Sasha Filosofov[107] with him. Masha went to Pirogovo with Philipp, the coachman. Tanya, Natasha, and Ilya went too, and are coming back to-morrow. Lyova growled and grumbled, and told us the sad story of how Ilya and Serezha had quarrelled —and over a mere horse.

In the evening I spent a little time copying Lyova's article on the Church.

The idea of the Church can no more be denied than true religion, which must guide all believers ; but the Church with all its present ritual is, of course, impossible. Why put a stick through a bit of bread instead of reading from the Gospel that the soldier pierced the side of Jesus ? And there are many other barbarous rites of this kind, which have killed the Church. It is ten o'clock now, and we are going to read aloud, and have tea. I haven't copied Lyova's diary to-day, and am feeling calmer and cleaner.

December 23.

These have been eventful days. The day before yesterday we were all wakened at six in the morning by the arrival of two telegrams. The first said that Sonya was ill ; the second that she had given birth to a son. I was very excited and happy, though not for long ; for I thought of Ilyusha—what a kind, good, but utterly unreliable father he will make ! I have always had an affection for Sonya, mainly because she is so very different from the restless, quarrelsome people that we all are—she is so gentle and meek. Ilya, Tanya, and Natasha Filosofov arrived by the Kursk train, and I had the usual unpleasant discussion with Ilya about property and money matters. He left yesterday evening. I spent the whole day in Tula, had dinner with the Davydovs, and did my Christmas shopping in a cheerless mood. It used to be so exciting in the old days, but now I am weary. The Filosofov girls left to-day, and later on Masha Kuzminsky and Erdelli arrived ; I made it clear to her that I didn't like her to be accompanied like this. I spent the day making flowers for the Christmas-tree and gilding nuts —and the day passed in an aimless sort of way. I got a very flattering and almost amorous letter from Fet, and I liked it, though I never loved him in the slightest, and even found him rather disagreeable.

December 27.

I got up late ; Vanichka came into my room, and I played with him for a whole hour. When I came down, I found that Serezha had arrived, and was playing the piano. He is so pleasant and good-humoured, and is a man who has done a sound piece of work and is now entitled to a rest. I find Masha Kuzminsky and Erdelli rather irritating ; they are neither one thing nor another ; they won't announce their engagement, and yet they behave as if they were engaged. My Masha is very thin and depressed—it worries me. All the children, Tanya, Lizzie, and I were busy making the Christmas pudding. We had a gay dinner, after which Lyova read from the Bible, and we laughed at all kinds of things. I cut out some cardboard dolls, and I am busy preparing a show for the children. It is silly. Dunayev has just arrived. It's late.

December 25.

Christmas : everybody is in a holiday mood. I've wasted my whole day on the Christmas tree. At breakfast Lyova and [little] Lyova had an exciting discussion about happiness, and the aims of life, though it began with a talk on altering the hours of our meals, and on the unsatisfactory aspects of *our* life. Lyova explained so clearly and intelligently to him that everything depended on one's self, on the *internal*, and not the *external* life. That is fine, only it gets annoying when he starts holding up his followers as models . . .* I am terribly afraid of becoming pregnant, for everybody will hear of this disgrace and gleefully repeat the recent Moscow joke—" *Voilà le véritable* ' *postscriptum* ' *de la Sonate de Kreutzer !* " The Christmas party went off well : we had about 80 village children at it ; we gave them a good time, and our own children were so happy and contented. For the first time I had a straight talk with Erdelli about his relations to Masha and their future marriage. They both look very miserable ; they are so anxious to get married, and yet something seems

* Thirty-seven words left out.

to be in their way. Lyova is cheerful and well, though he still keeps complaining of his digestion.

December 27.

I didn't write my diary yesterday. I don't like holidays and all the idleness and bustle and everybody's one desire to—enjoy themselves. I spent all day drawing and cutting out dolls ; I want to have a marionette show for the little ones. In the evening I grew sad at the thought how stupidly the day had passed. I had toothache and couldn't sleep at night. This morning I took up Rod's *Le Sens de la Vie*, and couldn't tear myself away from it for the rest of the day. What a subtle, delicate, and intelligent attitude to all the problems of life ! How simply, truthfully, and unaffectedly he treats all the serious and complicated questions of our everyday existence. The style is excellent, too. This has at last aroused all my interest in everything vital and spiritual. I suddenly felt capable of taking courage and creating a spiritual world of my own, which would be unaffected by Lyova's depressing sermons. In the evening the servants came in all dressed up in fancy costumes and danced to the piano and concertina. This was Tanya's doing, for she had been anxious to have some really *silly* fun. She and Masha dressed up also. But when Masha came in, Lyova and I simply gasped. She was wearing a pair of boy's breeches which were far too tight behind and were thoroughly indecent—where was her sense of shame ? A stupid, absurd, and utterly senseless idea. These boisterous parties always have a depressing effect on me. I retired to my room and opened the window, looking out at the stars and the clear, frosty sky, and suddenly remembered poor U.[1] It made me unbearably sad to realise that he was dead, that never again would I enjoy that pure, delicate relationship which was undoubtedly more than mere friendliness, and yet left not the slightest shadow of remorse, but filled so many years of my life with happiness. But who has need of my life now ? And who will give me care and affection—little Vanichka perhaps, but who else ? Yet thank God for that at least.

December 28, 1890.

The latter part of Rod's book is disappointing. His chapter on " Religion " is vague, and I don't believe he has actually found that solution, that *sens de la vie* for which I have been searching. But none of us have found it, and *never* will. It is the search for it which *is* life. And afterwards the God-Origin from whom we come will once again take us back. No one can live without that constant sense of the divine within one. I never take a single step without saying in my heart : O Lord, help me ; O Lord, forgive me ; O Lord have mercy on me. . . . And yet I know that my life is far from holy, though all the time I keep thinking : *now* is the moment to begin to be kind to everybody ; *now* the whole world around me will become a world of happiness and kindness. But I cannot do it. I keep watching Lyova ; there is so much in him ; such talent and intelligence, and yet so little of the sense of self-preservation ; everything excites and tortures and worries him. He was the same in his youth, and when he got married he still succeeded in keeping his mind and thoughts completely isolated; he had no family when he was young, and this lack of a family sense has lasted all through his life.

I had to find out something for Alexandrine Tolstoy yesterday, and I read over some of Lyova's letters to me. There was a time when he loved me so much that I saw in him my whole world, and looked for *him* in every child we had. I wonder now if it was only a physical matter to him, something which disappeared as time went on, leaving behind only a void. Yesterday in the drawing-room he talked to [young] Lyova of the difficulty he had in finding the right form for the *Kreutzer Sonata*. It was Andreyev Bulgakov, an actor and wonderful story-teller, who had suggested the narrative form to him. He also told Lyova about a man in a train who had told him the unhappy story of his wife's unfaithfulness, and Lyova at once made use of this story. He isn't so well to-day; he has a pain in his side, and his digestion is bad.

I spent all day copying out Lyova's diaries, and spent the evening talking in a most friendly way with all the family. We were expecting visitors from Tula —the Davydovs, the Lopukhins, and the Pisarevs, but no one came.

It is cold and windy—twelve degrees of frost.

December 29.

A lovely sunny winter day. The sky is blue, the trees are covered with hoar-frost, and the air is motionless. We spent nearly the whole day out of doors. The boys and girls went on their sleighs, and Masha K., Erdelli,[108] Lyova, and I skated. My skating is timid and poor ; all the same, it gives me a wonderfully soothing feeling. The Zinovievs came for dinner, with Mme. Giuliani and her little boy. The Zinovievs are pleasant, well-informed people. Luba played quite well, but still in a school-room fashion, so that no one got any pleasure out of it. Mme. Giuliani sang solos, and duets with Nadya. There is much passion in her singing—and probably in her character, too. Lyova is not very well ; he is quiet and unsociable. Serezha is going to see the Olsufievs. Tanya is unnaturally gay.

December 30.

I spent all the forenoon with Vanya, as nurse had gone to see her mother.

I finished reading Rod, and his prayer has become sincere and understandable to my mind. After dinner, Misha and Andryusha were getting the puppet show ready. I am mentally asleep. We spent the evening together, and talked about music in a calm, friendly way. [Young] Lyova went to a party in the village.

December 31.

I am so used to living not my own life, but the life of Lyova and the children, that I feel I have wasted my day if I haven't done something for them. I have again begun to copy Lyova's diaries. It is sad that my emotional dependence on the man I love should have killed so much of my energy and ability ; there was certainly once a great deal of energy in me.

I have done the accounts, although the money received and spent during the past twenty months doesn't tally. But it doesn't worry me ; I know how careless I am in noting down the expenses. I had a wire from Ilya asking me to be godmother. Sophie Andreyevna has refused, so has Tanya, so they are asking me, *faute de mieux*. But I don't mind ; I am more interested in my little grandson than in the people around, and I shall be glad to do it. I am leaving to-night, or, rather, early on New Year's Day —at five in the morning. I spent the afternoon with the children, copying. They are quiet and friendly to each other. We shall just celebrate the New Year among ourselves.

January 2, 1891.

I have come back from Ilya's, where I christened the baby. The Renunciation from Satan was as unimpressive as usual. But the baby, with his closed eyes and the happy, contented expression, and his little red face filled with the mystery of his soul and his future life, made me pray for him. Grinevka swarmed with members of the Filosofov family, all equally fat and good-natured. There is much of that good, sincere simplicity in their manners, with nothing spiteful or insincere. Ilya looked lost and bewildered, all the time fussing over trifles and unable to concentrate. It was sad to come home, for nobody seemed to pay the slightest attention to the fact that I had returned. I often wonder why they don't love me, and why I love them so much. It must be because of my outbursts of temper, when I become disagreeable and say unpleasant things. They all came in later on, but no one had even troubled to prepare something for me to eat ; but that didn't matter. Only Vanya was overjoyed to see me back, and Sasha, too, showed some pleasure, in her own gentle way. I found Kolya Gé and Pastukhov here. I was glad to see the former ; for I always like his genial face and kind heart. Misha isn't very well. The Davydovs came, and I tried to entertain them, but I'm afraid they were bored. I like him, and am always glad to see him.

I had a little row with Masha just now, about Birukov. She is trying to get in touch with him again, and I still cannot change my mind on the subject. If she marries him, it will be her death. I was very sharp and unfair, but I simply cannot discuss the matter calmly, and Masha is certainly a curse of God. She has given me nothing but pain ever since the day she was born. She is a stranger to the family, a stranger to God; and her imaginary love for Birukov is a puzzle to me.

January 3.

I spent my whole day over the puppet show. I filled the whole room with children, but the show was a failure. It's a pity that they should have liked Punch best when he was fighting. What savage, barbarous manners ! I am tired and bored. Pastukhov and young Gé are still here. Lyova is cheerful, and spent all morning writing about the Church. I can't get used to his philosophic and religious articles, and will always love him best as an artist. There is a blizzard outside, and seven degrees of frost.

January 7, 1891.

A terrible blizzard, and ten degrees of frost. The wind is howling in the chimneys, and there is deep snow all round the house. This morning we had a bad piece of news—Roman, one of our woodmen, was drunk last night and drove into the lake ; he got soaked, and Yakov Kurnosenkov, a peasant, had to take him home ; but the horse got drowned. It was a young horse—it is a great pity. Roman rushed home in a state of great excitement. Berger, our factor, has also gone off somewhere ; he is always telling lies and is terribly lazy—I am greatly dissatisfied with him. Masha has bought a tub, and now washes her own clothes. I told her she would ruin her health, as she had ruined mine already, but she took it very calmly. All the four young ones have colds, but they are up and about and are in good spirits. I wonder where Serezha can be, in this snowstorm. He went to see the Olsufievs ; I hope he didn't come away. Lyova has been complaining that he is unable to write. I spent all day tidying the house, and I also sorted some letters. I could die quite peacefully now ; everything is in such order. I am feeling quite ill with my palpitations, sickness, and difficult breathing, and I have a pain in my back as well. It's terrible to think that all these may be symptoms of pregnancy. It would be no wonder . . .* Lyova is very affectionate, and keeps thinking of me and all my work. If only our relations could be the same *without that* ! But it very seldom happens otherwise with him.

[Young] Lyova went out with the factor to look for the horse, but they lost their way and came back without finding it. He is very precious to me, and I am worried at his thinness and his state of depression. However, he looks much calmer now—and that makes me glad.

* Eight words left out.

January 5.

I am feeling ill—my back aches, my nose has been bleeding, one of my front teeth is aching, and I am afraid it may fall out—it would be disgusting to have to put in a false one. I've been copying Lyova's diary ever since the morning ; then I tidied his study and his clothes and linen. I took away some socks to mend, for he said that some of them had holes—and so I spent the forenoon. Then I played about with Vanichka for a while. Lyova and Gé went to see Bulygin, and Vanya and Petya Rayevsky arrived. I went on mending the socks, it is a nuisance, but I'll have to do it until I buy some new ones. In the evening I lost my temper with Misha because he had been beating Sasha. I rather overdid it ; I hit him on the back and made him kneel down in front of everybody. He began to cry, and ran off to his room. I felt sorry for him, for we are very fond of one another ; but he soon got over it. Masha Kuzminsky read to me Erdelli's letter. He is worried because of a lot of unpleasant gossip : what a pity that they should have all this unnecessary worry ! It's past one o'clock, but I am not sleepy. Lyova is very good to me, and it gives me great joy. I notice I've been very irritable lately, and have been too apt to lose my temper. I shouldn't be like this ; I'll have to be more careful ; but it's all the effect of my illness.

January 6.

I am still unwell : pains in the back and headache, and I can't sleep at night. I spent the day in a state of torpor, mending Lyova's socks. I've been sent a copy of Spinoza, but can't read it now, until my sight and my head get a little clearer ; at present I keep seeing black spots. Bulygin and Kolya Gé are here. Serezha arrived by the express train, and is happy and cheerful; we talked about trifles and about business and his visit to the Olsufievs. He is going on to Nikolskoye at night.

Misha and Andryusha went to the party in the village, but they don't seem to have enjoyed themselves : the village boys were shy and wouldn't play, and I am sorry they got no fun out of it. Masha keeps worrying me ; she and a village girl now go round visiting typhus cases ; I am afraid she will catch it and bring it into the house, and I told her so. It's a good thing to help the sick—I have always done it myself—but she never has any sense of proportion. But I spoke to her quite gently to-day, and felt terribly sorry for her, and was sad to think that we must always be strangers to one another. Lyova read his article on the Church to Gé, Bulygin, and [young] Lyova. I copied and read part of it. But I still can't develop any liking for these dogmatic, religious, non-artistic articles ; they offend me and destroy something within me, and fill me with vague alarm.

January 7, 1981.

I have been thinking all morning of the phrase Masha used yesterday when she spoke of marrying Birukov—" I'll go potatoing "—those were her words, meaning that she would go and plant potatoes. I have now adopted the habit of never answering right away. but of thinking things over and giving my opinion the next day. After considering the matter, I sent Birukov the money to-day for the book he had sent Masha, and told him of my unwillingness to see her marry him, asking him not to come here, and not to write to her. Masha overheard me telling Lyova about the letter, and said she would cancel all the promises she had ever made to me, and the tears came to my eyes, too, with all the excitement. Masha is certainly a sad problem to me, with her insincerity, and her imaginary love for Birukov, and she has been a problem all her life.

This morning Lyova went to Pirogovo with Mitrokha. Tanya went to Tula for the day, and had all her money stolen ; and somebody also stole two cartloads of wood from the shed through the night. I copied L.'s diaries in the morning. Then I helped the children with their lessons and mended socks—but I can do no more. What an infernal labour ! In the evening they read aloud two dull and disgusting stories which that stupid, senseless Chertkov had sent. Kolya Gé, who left with Bulygin last night, hasn't yet returned. What a wonderfully kind and clever man ! There is something joyous about his calm serenity. He must have had a painful, harassing time before he attained his present way of living. He did not deceive himself into thinking that this life held only good, but took it as it came, serenely and calmly, saying to himself : " There is only one life to live, and the past will never come back." It is quite true. Masha Kuzminsky has lost all personality. Erdelli has absorbed her whole mind, and the rest of the world has ceased to exist for her.

I have been thinking to-day that nine-tenths of all the happenings in this world have a certain motive of love behind them ; but people carefully conceal this, because it would mean revealing the most intimate passions and feelings and thoughts. I could name many such instances, but it is as fearsome as physical nakedness. But in Lyova's diaries there is no *love*, as I understand it ; this feeling was evidently unknown to him. He only knew sensuality . . .* However, that happened in the Caucasus. But it is none the less revolting. I don't think I have made my thought clear about love as a motive. I mean that if a man is seized with a feeling of love—he puts it in everything : into his life and work, into his relation towards others, into his books, and the joy and energy he puts into it all is so powerful that it inspires all the people around him. That is why I can't understand Masha Kuzminsky's love. She seems to be depressed—but perhaps it has been going on too long.

January 8.

I have been flooded with work ever since morning. I've been looking through the books and accounts connected with Yasnaya Polyana and the timber. Then Gé and I read the proofs of the thirteenth volume of the new edition of the collected works. Then I taught Andryusha and Misha music for two solid hours. After dinner, I wrote some chords for the children, and counted up the cost of butter and eggs. Then I drafted an application about my case against the Ovsiannikovo priest, and about the transfer of the Grinevka estate. I seem to have been putting everything in order—perhaps I am going to die soon ? I really ought to go to Moscow to see about this thirteenth volume, but I don't feel like it. I am feeling

* Fourteen words left out.

sad—though for no reason : everybody is well and happy, thank God. Sasha and Vanichka and I said our prayers together. Tanya, Masha, and Kolya Gé have gone off to Kozlovka. I haven't been seeing much of Lyova ; he is busy downstairs reading and writing. I hardly ever see him except when he is eating or sleeping. He is well and happy.

January 9.

I was less energetic to-day, though I got up shortly after nine. I felt too lazy to do much copying, and gave Misha only one lesson. Then I showed Andryusha how to play duets ; then we had dinner ; and after dinner I wrote for a little, and read Zasodimsky's story, *The Flickering Hearth*, which is quite well written and even moved me to tears. Tanya and I played the Kreutzer Sonata, arranged as a piano duet, but it went badly : it's far too hard to play without previous practice. Andryusha had toothache in the evening. I carried Vanichka about in my arms ; he had a sore throat. What an affectionate, loving, clever, delicate little boy he is ! I love him too much, and I am afraid he won't live. I often dream of having another boy, and am worried in case I am pregnant. My letter to *Le Figaro* has been translated and published in the *Russkie Vedomosti* : but there are some mis-translations in it, and the word *reputation* looks very awkward in the Russian. I wrote letters to my sister Tanya and to old Gé, and am going to bed now. I have got the document, plans, and money all ready, and am going to Tula to-morrow.

January 10.

I got up at ten, and didn't go to Tula because of the terrible wind. I cut out some clothes for Sasha, did some copying, and gave much energy to the children's music lesson and to Andryusha's lesson on the Church service. He is so obstinate and absent-minded, and seems purposely *not* to understand what I say. The more heart I put into it, the more rude and absent-minded he gets. How he tortures me ! What a hard time the poor boy will have with such a character. After dinner the three girls drove to Yasenki to meet the express train by which Erdelli was to arrive ; he is going on to see his mother. He and Masha spent the evening cooing like a pair of doves. We read Soloviev's article on Fet and on lyrical poetry ; rather clever, but one-sided. We also listened to a rather silly story. Later on, Lyova and Nikolai Nikolaevich played chess with Alexander Mitrofanovich, who, much to our surprise, played without watching the moves. I wrote a letter to my brother Vyacheslav. Lyova is well and very cheerful and lively . . .*

We talked about the censorship and how it prevented writers from expressing their most important beliefs, but I maintained that, quite apart from that, there was such a thing as free and purely artistic literature against which the censor was helpless, and I gave *War and Peace* as an example. Lyova said peevishly that he had renounced those books,[109] and I believe he is so aggressive because *The Kreutzer Sonata* has been prohibited. He talked of it during the evening.

* Thirty-six words left out.

January 12.

I went to Tula yesterday, where I cashed the coupons, sent in the application for the Grinevka transfer, paid the accounts, and had a particularly unpleasant time with the priest's wife over the disputed land. I walked four times from the district court to the provincial office and back, for they kept sending me from one office to another, saying that my business had nothing to do with them. In the end, I left without getting anything settled. Not for long have I been so depressed as I was yesterday, when I waited in the counsel's room for my solicitor, who was late in coming. It is hard to do all this business ; it would be so much easier to say : I am a Christian and shan't do anything, for it goes against my rules ! But I must get someone to go to Tula instead of me ; for I can't go on doing this. There was a terrible wind, almost a hurricane, and I was very tired . . .*

I dropped in at the Davydovs for a minute ; Chelokaeva was there ; I like her for her intelligence and worldly wisdom. It was Misha's name-day party, and the dinner was waiting when I got home. Vanichka was so delighted to see me come back. At three in the morning he developed a temperature and began to cough, and, though I didn't want to get up, I finally had to, and spent some time with him, trying to soothe him. I got up late this morning, and, although it was Tanya's name-day, I gave the children their lessons. Andryusha played quite well, but Misha merely frowned and was very obstinate. [Young] Lyova and Vera Tolstoy came back from Pirogovo. Vanya and Petya Rayevsky arrived in the middle of dinner.

* Seven words left out.

Everybody was in a holiday mood ; all the children played games, and Vanichka was delighted. He hasn't been allowed to run around all day, but, though he is coughing and has fever, he is still quite bright and cheerful. Later, everybody went as far as Kozlovka to see Kolya Gé off. A letter came from Vera Nagornov, and the proofs of *The Kreutzer Sonata*. The thing is coming to a *dénouement*. I wonder what will happen ? Will it be banned, or not—and what shall I do ?

I haven't a moment for reading or writing, or anything. To-morrow I must go over the proofs, and cut out some more clothes. I am feeling very lonely and sad.

January 13.

Vanichka is ill ; he didn't get up at twelve, and had as much as 39·4 by 2 o'clock,* and it was the same at nine at night. He coughed at night, and the thick phlegm in his little throat made it difficult for him to breathe. He had a cold in the head, and in the morning his ear began to hurt. I felt so sorry for him, and it was so exhausting. All the rest of the time I was busy correcting the proofs of volume thirteen, which includes *The Kreutzer Sonata*. Masha Kuzminsky helped me. Vera Tolstoy went away, and the girls saw her off. Lyova and [young] Lyova went to Kozlovka in the evening. It is twenty-four below zero. While Vanichka was choking last night, I ran into Masha's room, to ask if she had an emetic. She was sleeping at the time, but quickly woke and jumped out of bed with the greatest eagerness to find some ipecacuanha ; as she turned to

* Centigrade.

me, her face looked so delicate, kind, appealing, that my first impulse was to put my arms round her and to kiss her. Wouldn't she have been surprised ! All day to-day I've been watching that same expression on her face, and I love her. If only I could keep up this feeling towards her—it would make me so happy ! I shall try.

January 14.

Vanichka is better ; his temperature went up to 38·5 during the day, but it fell later on ; his cough is less and he is once more quite cheerful. [Young] Lyova went off to Moscow, and Klopsky has arrived.[110] He is one of the " dark ones," and is extremely repulsive. I answered Misha Stakhovich's and Varya Nagornov's letters, and copied for a short time ; later on I instructed Andryusha in the liturgy and Misha in Holy Communion. After dinner I spent some time with Vanichka and then copied some more of Lyova's diary (I have now reached 1854), and then sat about downstairs with the girls. My brain is completely asleep. In the evening we helped Mitrokha to get ready for his journey to Moscow ; Andryusha and Misha were greatly excited, and gave him 50 roubles of their own money and an overcoat. The frost is terrible. Lyova is peevish and irritable. I am always so afraid of his merciless sarcasm. I have become terribly sensitive to it.

January 15.

It's a hard struggle at times. This morning the children were doing their lessons downstairs, and that Klopsky man was there. He suddenly said to

Andryusha : " Why are you studying and killing your souls ? Don't you know that your father doesn't want it ? " The girls were delighted and were almost prepared to shake his noble hand for such words. But the boys came running to me to tell me all about it. It was very difficult to show them that mental work alone justified our aristocratic existence, and that if one did neither mental work nor peasants' work one was in danger of remaining completely idle ; that I alone was responsible for their education, and that if they didn't study properly the shame of it would fall on me, and I would be much grieved if all my labours were wasted.

January 16.

I had to go to Tula again on business, and spent the day rushing around and seeing crowds of people and talking endlessly. I saw about the Grinevka transfer, the dispute with the Ovsiannikovo priest, and the sale of timber. I also had Peter Vassilyevich's passport straightened out. I called on the Rayevskys, and had dinner at the Zinovievs. Their little Manya is very like my Vanichka ; she sat on my knee and kept kissing my cheek. On my way home I kept praying and thinking of all my enemies, and decided to write a kind letter to Birukov—which I did. I decided to come to a friendly settlement with the priest's wife, and wrote to her also to that effect. I also answered Baroness Ixkull's letter in which she asked permission to print *Kholstomer* and *Polikushka* in a popular edition. I refused the one, but agreed to the other. I further wrote to Serezha and sent him the title-deed regarding the transfer of Grinevka. Everyone at home was in high spirits—

just as might be expected. I also decided to get Masha to help the families of the peasants who will be sent to jail on account of the stolen timber.

January 17.

I got up late, and in a lazy mood. I was tired after yesterday's trip. I wrote to [young] Lyova, copied the diary, and finished the Caucasian section. I tutored Andryusha on the Church service, and gave them both a music lesson which lasted two whole hours. They worked well and willingly. I did some more copying after dinner, and spent some time with Vanichka, who was crying with earache. Later on we read aloud a rather dull French novel. At dinner we had a flippant talk about what would happen if the masters and servants changed places for a week. Lyova frowned and went downstairs ; I went after him and asked what the matter was. He said : " I don't like this stupid talk about a sacred subject ; it causes me quite enough pain to be surrounded by servants, and when one starts making jokes about it, especially in front of the children, I find it very unpleasant." I tried to calm him. At the same time, he has just been arguing, with much irritation, with Alexei Mitrofanovich, trying to defend Strakhov.

January 18.

I am unwell ; every muscle in my stomach is sore, and I have a slight temperature. I had a terrible row with Nurse ; she had been rude ever since yesterday, and takes no care of the baby ; but to-day, feeling ill, I lost my temper altogether, and told her that I wouldn't stand any impertinence from a low-down hussy. Here she became so thoroughly objectionable that, if it hadn't been for my silly love for Vanichka, I would have dismissed her on the spot. The poor little boy realised at once that something was wrong, and, clinging to my skirt, he kept saying, " Mummy's good, Mummy's good." If only people were all like children ! I coached Misha, copied, groaned, couldn't eat anything, but didn't go to bed after all. Lyova's diaries about Sebastopol, and the Crimean War are very interesting. But one torn-out page struck me specially with its coarse, filthy cynicism. Yes, I simply cannot reconcile the ideas of woman's *marriage* and man's debauchery. Marriage cannot be happy after the husband's debauchery. It is a constant wonder to me that we have kept it up so long. What saved our marriage was my childlike innocence and my instinct of self-preservation. I instinctively closed my eyes on his past, and deliberately refrained from reading these diaries and from questioning him about his past. Otherwise it would have been the end for us both. He doesn't realise that my purity alone saved us from perdition. But it's perfectly true. His cold-blooded debauchery, and his views on the subject, and all these pictures of a voluptuous life are a poison which could easily have ruined a woman who was even slightly infatuated with somebody else. " So that's what you were like ; you have soiled me with your past—just let me pay you back ! " That's what most women would feel after reading these diaries.

January 19.

I am still ill—my stomach and feverish condition are the same. As if in a dream, I taught the children music for two hours and corrected the long proof of *The Kreutzer Sonata*. It amazes me how much good work I can do. Only it's a pity that I never had an opportunity of applying my abilities to something higher and worthier than mere mechanical labour. If only I could paint or write stories ! I got a wonderful letter from [young] Lyova—but, heavens ! how gloomy and impressionable he is ! When there is no joy in life, there is no unity or harmony either in one's life or labours. It's a pity.

There is such an obvious thread connecting the early diaries with *The Kreutzer Sonata* : and a buzzing fly is struggling in the web—and the spider has sucked its blood . . .

January 20.

I am feeling better, but have still got a cold. Misha caught the grippe, but Sasha and Vanya are better. Erdelli has come. His mother won't allow him to marry Masha for at least three years. Masha is terribly upset, and so, I believe, is he. We all cried ; and I felt extremely sorry for them, but couldn't advise them what to do. He is a poor, miserable boy. The children played after dinner, while the girls and I did some writing. I read some Spinoza before dinner, but don't quite grasp him yet, though I find his explanation of God entirely satisfactory and in full agreement with my own conceptions. I read a bit of a French novel. Later on the last set of proofs of *The Kreutzer Sonata* arrived, and I read it, thank God, without the old excitement, and made only one correction. Lyova doesn't sleep well and is unable to write. It was warmer in the morning—one and a half below zero —but now it has dropped to seven again.

January 23, 1891.

I haven't written my diary for three days. The day before yesterday we had visitors—Mme. Rayevsky, Erdelli, and Alexander Alexandrovich Behrs. The day passed in a futile manner, and I was stupidly effusive. Lyova walked all the way to Tula yesterday ; it was a warm day, and, as Rayevsky had come all the way in the morning to join his wife, this tempted Lyova to try it, too. He had dinner with the Zinovievs (Zinoviev himself was away), and spent the evening with the Rayevskys. He came back by train along with Alexei Mitrofanovich. Serezha was in Tula too, and came to see us to-day ; the three of us—he, Tanya, and I—sat together and had a long talk about family life, and the Erdelli business, and things in general. He left after dinner. I worked with the sewing machine. My eyes and head are all aching with the cold. Everyone in the home has got the grippe. This illness makes me quite dazed.

NOTES

NOTES *

" The trip to Troitza " is the only surviving fragments of Countess Tolstoy's diarie written before her wedding. She destroyed the rest in 1862.

1. Lubov (Luba) Alexandrovna Behrs (1842–1920), a first cousin of Countess Tolstoy's.

2. The two Lisas were Elizaveta Andreyevna Behrs (1843–1919), Countess Tolstoy's eldest sister, and Elizaveta Alexandrovna Behrs, a cousin (1835–99).

3. Alexander (Sasha) Andreyevich Behrs (1845–1918), one of the author's brothers.

4. Troitze-Sergievo, a famous Russian monastery, about fifty miles from Moscow, founded in the fourteenth century.

5. Vladimir Andreyevich Behrs (1853–74), another brother of the author.

6–7. Alexander Mikhailovich Islenyev (1794–1882), Countess Tolstoy's maternal grandfather. Was married to Sophie Petrovna Kozlovsky, who died in 1830, and later to Sophie Alexandrovna Zhdanov (1812–80). He had three daughters by his second marriage—Aglaya (born 1844 ; died young) ; Olga (1844–1909) ; and Nathalie (born 1847). Countess Tolstoy was particularly friendly with Olga.

8. Maria (Masha) Nikolaevna Tolstoy (1830–1912) was Tolstoy's only sister. She married, in 1847, her second cousin, Valerian Petrovich Tolstoy, but left him in 1857 and went abroad. She spent two winters (1861–2 and 1862–3) in Algiers. In 1861 she married a Swedish nobleman, after whose death, in 1874, she became a nun.

9. Tatyana (Tanya) Andreyevna Behrs (1846–1925), Countess Tolstoy's youngest sister. She married A. M. Kuzminsky in 1867. L. Tolstoy was very fond of her, and modelled on her his Natasha Rostov (*War and Peace*). For many years after her marriage she spent the summers in Yasnaya Polyana, together with her husband and children.

10. Tatyana Alexandrovna Ergolsky (1795–1874), a second cousin of Tolstoy's father. After the death of Tolstoy's mother, she devoted herself to his upbringing. Tolstoy was deeply devoted to her, and considered her as one of the most important influences of his childhood and youth.

11. Prince Nicholas Sergeyevich Volkonsky (1753–1821), Tolstoy's maternal grandfather. He is the original of Prince Nicholas Andreyevich Bolkonsky of *War and Peace*.

12. Count Nicholas Ilyich Tolstoy (1795–1837), Tolstoy's father. Had a military career, and took part in the wars of 1812 and 1813. He married Princess Marie Nikolayevna Volkonsky in 1822. Tolstoy's father and mother are the originals of Nicholas Rostov and Marie Bolkonsky in *War and Peace*.

13. This episode is almost literally reproduced in *Anna Karenina*.

14. Andrey Evstafyevich Behrs (1808–68), Countess Tolstoy's father. He had a distinguished medical and civil service career. Countess Tolstoy's brothers were the following : Alexander (1845–1918) ; Peter (1849–1910) ; Vladimir (1853–74) ; Stepan (1855–1909), who wrote a book of reminiscences on Tolstoy ; legal career ; Vyacheslav (1861–1907), a distinguished engineer.

---

*These are based on the notes in the Russian edition compiled by S. L. Tolstoy and G. A. Volkov.

15. The search in Yasnaya Polyana took place on July 7, 1862, during Tolstoy's absence. The teachers of the Yasnaya Polyana school were suspected of keeping an illegal printing press in Tolstoy's house ; nothing, however, was found.

16. Feodor Timofeyevich Stellovsky, a Moscow publisher and music-seller who published Tolstoy's works in two volumes in 1864.

17. Sergei Nikolaevich Tolstoy (1826–1904), L. Tolstoy's brother, with whom he was very friendly all his life. S. N. married Marie (Masha) Nikolaevna Shishkin (1829–1919) in 1867, after living with her for eighteen years.

18. Alexander Mikhailovich Islenyev and Sophie Petrovna Kozlovsky were not legally married ; their son, therefore, did not bear his father's name, but the invented name of Islavin, though Countess Tolstoy refers to him as Isleneyev.

19. Tolstoy accomplished his plan of writing books for children. His A B C was published in four parts in 1872. Some of the *byliny* and folk-tales referred to by Countess Tolstoy are included in the book.

20. Afanasi Afanasyevich Fet (1820–92), the famous lyrical poet, one of the few literary contemporaries with whom Tolstoy was intimate before his "conversion."

21. Lieutenant Mirovich, executed for his attempt to liberate from the Schlüsselburg Fortress Ioann Antonovich, a pretender to the Throne (1741).

22. The woman referred to is obviously Anna Karenina.

23. Sergei (Serezha) Lvovich Tolstoy, Tolstoy's eldest son, born June 28, 1863. The editor of the Russian text of the present *Diary*.

24. The *Chetyi-Minei*, a Russian mediæval Church " almanack " composed of the lives of the Russian saints in calendar order.

25. The " failure " of the A B C was only temporary. The second edition, which appeared in 1874, had a very considerable success. According to the Russian editors of the *Diary*, " a few generations of Russians learned to read and write from Tolstoy's A B C."

26. Alexei Mikhailovich (1629–76), the second Tsar of the Romanov dynasty ; father of Peter the Great.

27. Ivan Nikolaevich Kramskoy (1839–87), the famous Russian portrait-painter. His well-known portrait of Tolstoy is at the Tretyakov Gallery in Moscow. Another version of the same portrait is still at Yasnaya Polyana.

28. Tatyana (Tanya) Lvovna Tolstoy, born October 4, 1864, Tolstoy's eldest daughter. She wrote a book of reminiscences (*Friends and Visitors in Yasnaya Polyana*), published in 1923.

29. The migration to thinly populated agricultural regions in the south east, in Siberia, etc., became very widespread during the fifteen or twenty years following the liberation of the serfs in 1861. The aim of this migration was largely the desire for *individual* ownership.

30. The work in question is *The Decembrists*. This novel was begun in 1863, but abandoned in favour of *War and Peace*. Later on, in 1877, Tolstoy returned to *The Decembrists*, and took it up again from a new standpoint, with the " expansion idea " as its centre. Only a few fragments of this novel were written (1877–8). These were published in Moscow in 1925.

31. Prince Alexei Pavlovich Bobrinsky, who advocated the belief that salvation was gained not so much by good deeds as by the faith in Christ. This doctrine was formed under the influence of Radstock's sermons.

32. The Russo-Turkish War of 1877–8.

33. The personal acquaintance between Tolstoy and Turgenev dates back to 1855, following Tolstoy's return from the Sebastopol Campaign. Turgenev had known Tolstoy's sister, Maria (see Note 8), long before that, and had spoken highly to her of her brother's early works.

NOTES

34. Grigori (Grisha) Sergeyevich Tolstoy (born 1853) was the son of Sergei, Lev Nikolaevich's brother, and his mistress, later his wife, Marie Shishkin (see Note 17). Countess Tolstoy pities him for not being a "real," i.e. a legitimate son. At that time his parents were not legally married.

35. Nikolskoye—Vyazemskoye, an estate about eighty miles distant from Yasnaya Polyana, which Tolstoy inherited after the death of his brother Nicholas in 1860.

36. The " students " were the teachers whom Tolstoy was employing in his Yasnaya Polyana school.

37. Nathalie Petrovna Okhotnitsky, a poor gentlewoman, who acted as companion to Tatiana Alexandrovna Ergolsky.

38. " Never so much in love " is an entry in Tolstoy's pre-marriage diary (May 10–13, 1858). The words refer to Axinya Anikanova, a peasant woman in Yasnaya Polyana, with whom Tolstoy was having an affair at the time.

39. A. M. Kusminsky, a cousin of Countess Tolstoy's, who married her sister, Tatyana (Tanya) Behrs, in 1867. He had a very distinguished legal career.

40. Valeria Vladimirovna Arsenyev (1836–1909). After the death of her father in 1853, Tolstoy was appointed her, her sister's, and her brother's guardian. In that capacity he often visited Sudakovo, five miles from Yasnaya Polyana. He was in love with Valeria in 1856–7, and intended to marry her. She married Anatoli Alexandrovich Talyzin in 1858.

41. About this time Tolstoy and Bibikov (the neighbour mentioned in connection with Anna Karenina's death) intended to build a distillery. The plan was abandoned, largely in view of Countess Tolstoy's opposition.

42. The young people were : Tatyana Behrs (Countess Tolstoy's sister), Alexander Behrs (her brother), Alexander Mikhailovich Kusminsky (see Note 39), Tatyana's future husband, and Anatoli Lvovich Shostak. Shostak courted Tatyana Behrs at the time, but, as he had evidently no intention of marrying her, he was asked to leave Yasnaya. (*Reminiscences of T. A. Kusminsky.*)

43. Soon after the birth of Countess Tolstoy's child she had an inflammation of the breast, which caused such pain that she was unable for a time to nurse the child, and hired a wet-nurse. Tolstoy protested against this on principle, and hence his quarrel with his wife. The " platitudes " were evidently his die-hard views on the subject.

44. The Behrs family expected Tolstoy to propose, not to Sophie Andreyevna, but to Elizaveta Andreyevna, her eldest sister, who was in love with him.

45. The " mad night," as Tolstoy called it in his diary, was a night of jealousy. Tolstoy was jealous of his wife because of A. A. Erlenwein, a teacher at the Yasnaya Polyana School.

46. This is the only existing reference to Tolstoy's desire to " go to war " in connection with the Polish Revolt of 1863. It must have been only a momentary fancy.

47. Countess Alexandra Andreyevna Tolstoy (1817–1904), a first cousin of Tolstoy's father, and Tolstoy's life-long friend.

48. A reference to *War and Peace* which Tolstoy began to write in the autumn of 1863, and on the material of which he was working for a long time before.

49. Alyosha Gorshok, a half-witted peasant at Yasnaya Polyana.

50. About this time Sergei Nikolaevich Tolstoy was courting Countess Tolstoy's sister, Tatyana Behrs. She accepted his proposal, but the engagement was soon broken off (see Note 17).

51. Apparently meaning Tatyana and Serezha, Countess Tolstoy's little son, not Serezha, Tatyana's fiancé.

NOTES

52. *The Zephyrotes*, a nickname given by Tolstoy to his nieces, the daughters of his sister Maria and Valerian Petrovich Tolstoy.

53. Gustav Keller, a German, whom Tolstoy engaged as a teacher for the Yasnaya school during his travels in Germany. He became, later on, the tutor of Grigory Sergeyevich Tolstoy (Tolstoy's nephew), and, later still, a German teacher at the Tula High School.

54. Pirogovo, Sergei Nikolaevich's estate, about twenty-five miles from Yasnaya.

55. Maria Nikolaevna Tolstoy (see Note 8) and her daughters Varvara (or Barbara) (1850–1921), married in 1872 to Nagornov, and Elizaveta (Elizabeth) (born 1852), married in 1871 to Prince Obolensky.

56. The Fets (see Note 20) lived on their estate of Novoselki, eleven miles from Nikolskoye, Tolstoy's other estate (see Note 35).

57. Count Vladimir Sollogub (1813–82), a well-known author. Tolstoy knew him since 1850.

58. Without warning his wife, Tolstoy had invited a military band to her name-day party. It was the band of a regiment stationed in the neighbourhood at the time.

59. Darya (Dasha) Alexandrovna Kusminsky, Tatyana Andreyevna's eldest daughter (Countess Tolstoy's niece).

60. Alexander Mikhailovich Kusminsky was appointed to an important Government post in Kutaiss.

61. Tolstoy went for his *kumiss* (fermented mare's milk) cure to the Samara region in June 1871, and returned to Yasnaya early in August.

62. Nicholas Mikhailovich Nagornov (1845–96) was married in 1872 to Varvara Valerianovna Tolstoy, the daughter of Maria Nikolaevna, Tolstoy's sister.

63. Marie (Masha) Lyovna Tolstoy, Tolstoy's daughter, was born on February 12, 1871, and died on November 23, 1906. Married Prince N. L. Obolensky in 1897.

64. Hannah Tardsey (born 1845), the daughter of a Windsor Palace gardener, entered the service of the Tolstoys in 1866. Owing to bad health, she went to the Caucasus in 1872, when she became the governess of Tatyana Andreyevna Kusminsky's children. Two years later she married a Caucasian prince.

65. Refers to *Anna Karenina*, which Tolstoy began to write on March 18, 1873.

66. Ippolit Mikhailovich Nagornov (or Nagornyi, as Countess Tolstoy erroneously calls him), the brother of Varvara Valerianovna's husband (see Note 62), was a virtuoso violinist who came to visit the Tolstoys during the summer of 1876.

67. M. Jules Rey (born 1848 (?)), a Catholic Swiss from Fribourg. Tutor to the three elder Tolstoy boys (1875–7).

68. Nicholas Valerianovich Tolstoy (1850–79), the son of Maria Nikolaevna, Tolstoy's sister. Married Nadezhda Feodorovna Gromov, the daughter of the Tula architect referred to in " L. N. Tolstoy's Marriage."

69. Dmitri Vasilyevich Ulyaninsky (1861–1918), while still at school himself, came to Yasnaya every week-end to coach Sergei Lvovich (Serezha) for his exams. He later became a well-known bibliographer, and committed suicide in 1918.

70. Anna Philipps, an English governess.

71. M. Nief, a tutor of the elder boys. A former *communard* of the Paris Commune of 1871, who had fled to Russia under the name of Nief. His real name was Montels. He stayed with the Tolstoys from December 1877 to October 1879.

NOTES

72. Prince Leonid Dmitrievich Urusov (died 1885) was Vice-Governor of the Tula Province from 1876 to 1885. He was a friend of the Tolstoys, and was platonically in love with Countess Tolstoy (see the remarkable tribute to his friendship in her entry of December 27, 1890).

73. Anton (1861–1919 ?), Rossa (born 1859), and Nadezhda (born 1863) Delvig, children of Baron Alexander Delvig, the brother of the poet Delvig, Pushkin's friend.

74 Alexander Grigoryevich Michurin, the son of a serf musician, and a musician himself. He taught the Tolstoy children music once a week.

75. Vasili Ivanovich Alexeyev (1848–1919), the son of a poor landowner and a peasant-woman. Graduated in mathematics at the University of Moscow and took part in Chaikovsky's *narodnik* movement. In 1875 he became a member of the Russian agricultural colony in Kansas, U.S.A., who practised moral self-perfection. He soon returned to Russia, and became a tutor to the elder children of the Tolstoys. Tolstoy was on very friendly terms with him, and they had a mutual influence on one another.

76. The novel referred to is *The Decembrists* (see Note 30).

77. Alexei Alexeyevich Bibikov (died 1914), the factor of the Tolstoy estates in the Samara region. (Not to be confused with Bibikov, their Yasnaya Polyana neighbour.)

78 Countess Tolstoy's biography of her husband appeared in Vol. IX. of the *Russian Library*, published in 1879. It is only five pages long.

79. *The Cossacks*. Translated by Eugene Schuyler, London, 1878. Schuyler had visited Yasnaya Polyana, and wrote some reminiscences relating to 1867–70.

80. Gill, the owner of coal-mines and of a large chemical and lime factory, some five miles from Yasnaya.

81. Prince D. D. Obolensky was very wealthy in his youth, but was ruined during the war of 1877, and became bankrupt.

82. Grigori, a butler.

83. Tolstoy bought this house (now a part of the Tolstoy Museum) for £3,800 during the summer of 1882. After repairing and rebuilding it, he moved into it with his family in the autumn of 1882.

84. Nicholas Mikhailovich Lopatin (1854–97), a singer and collector of Russian folk-songs. Tolstoy was greatly interested in his song collections.

85. Konstantin Zyabrev (died 1895), a poor and inefficient villager. Tolstoy once helped him to re-thatch his hut. He wrote some reminiscences of Tolstoy.

86. Ganya, a village pauper.

87. Alexander Petrovich Ivanov (died 1911), a retired artillery lieutenant who spent much of his life wandering about Russia. In 1880 he " dropped in " at Yasnaya, and Tolstoy engaged him as a copyist. He left soon after, but used to come back again. He was addicted to drink to a disastrous degree.

88. *The Powers of Darkness*, a play in five acts, was written during October and November 1886.

89. Isaac Borisovich Feinemann (1862–1925), a Jew; an extreme disciple of Tolstoy's. He settled down in the Yasnaya village, worked for the peasants, and gave away all he had to anyone who asked him. In the meantime, Countess Tolstoy supported his wife. He later turned Orthodox, and has written, under the name of Teneromo, some personal reminiscences of Tolstoy. His facts are very doubtful.

NOTES

90. N. N. Gé (1831–94), the famous Russian painter, and friend of Tolstoy's. He painted several portraits of the Tolstoy family.

90A. Vladimir Grigoryevich Chertkov (born 1854), son of General-Lieutenant Grigori Chertkov, and an ex-officer himself, was one of the most influential of Tolstoy's followers. He became, during the last ten years of Tolstoy's life, the leader of the group hostile to Tolstoy's family. Tolstoy in his will made Chertkov his literary editor and executor.

91. Ilya Lvovich, Tolstoy's second son, was serving his term in the army at the time.

92. N. N. Gé (born 1857), the son of the painter, collaborated with Countess Tolstoy in preparing Tolstoy's works for the press.

93. The letter to Engelhardt, dealing with non-resistance, was first published in Christchurch in 1904. It was not officially published in Russia until 1911, but its contents was widely known long before that date.

94. George Kennan, the American traveller and author of *Siberia and the Exile System* (London, 1891). Kennan visited Yasnaya Polyana twice.

95. Sophie Nikolayevna Filosofov (born 1867) was then engaged to Ilya Tolstoy, whom she married in February 1888.

96. N. N. Strakhov (1828–96), the well-known critic and philosopher, and friend of Tolstoy's and Dostoevsky's.

97. P. D. Golokhvastov (1838–92), a writer and scholar of old Russian poetry.

98. Pavel Ivanovich Birukov (born 1860), Tolstoy's friend and the author of his standard four-volume biography.

99. Stepan Andreich Behrs, Countess Tolstoy's brother, and his wife, a former provincial actress.

100. Sophie Alexeyevna's Filosofov, the mother of Ilya Tolstoy's wife.

101. Ivan (Vanya or Vanichka) Tolstoy (1888–95), Tolstoy's youngest son, the favourite of the family.

102. The need for physical work was part of Tolstoy's new creed ; in 1887 he learned to make boots. This is a reference to his shoemaking activities.

103. The editors of the Russian text doubt that Tolstoy should have advised his wife to " give the peasants a fright." All discussions relating to the protection of his property were always extremely unpleasant to him.

104. E. Dillon (born 1854), an Irishman, Professor of Comparative Philology at the University of Kharkov during the early eighties, correspondent of the *Daily Telegraph*, and translator of some of Tolstoy's stories.

105. Evgeni Ivanovich Popov (born 1864), one of Tolstoy's followers. He wrote some mathematical and scientific books and essays, including one on vegetarianism. Countess Tolstoy calls him an " Asiatic," because his mother was Caucasian.

106. P. G. Khokhlov (1864–96), a fervent Tolstoyan. Died in an asylum.

107. Sasha is Alexandra Nikolaevna Filosofov, the sister of Ilya Tolstoy's wife.

108. With Tatyana Lvovna and Marie Lvovna. The " Kuzminsky girls " are the daughters of Tatyana Andreyevna, Sophie Andreyevna's sister. One of them, Masha, married Ivan Yegorovich Erdelli in 1891.

109. In the autumn of 1884, Tolstoy handed his wife a full power of attorney relating to all his property and to the works written prior to 1881.

110. Klopsky (1852–189—), the son of a church deacon, a fanatical Tolstoyan. He gave the impression of an insane person. He emigrated to America, and was killed there in a street accident.

THE END

www.ingramcontent.com/pod-product-compliance
Lightning Source LLC
Chambersburg PA
CBHW022118080426
42734CB00006B/179
* 9 7 8 1 4 3 4 4 2 2 0 8 8 *